中国之租借地

ZHONGGUO ZHI ZUJIEDI

陶行知硕士论文（英汉）

陶行知　著
张汉敏　周洪宇　译

·南京·

图书在版编目（CIP）数据

中国之租借地：陶行知硕士论文：汉文、英文 / 陶行知著；张汉敏，周洪宇译 . —— 南京：东南大学出版社，2022.12
（陶行知师德师风系列丛书）
ISBN 978-7-5766-0361-3

Ⅰ.①中… Ⅱ.①陶… ②张… ③周… Ⅲ.①租借地 – 中外关系 – 国际关系史 – 文集 – 汉、英 Ⅳ.① D829.12-53

中国版本图书馆 CIP 数据核字（2022）第 232215 号

Courtesy of the University of Illinois at Urbana-Champaign Archives.
原文为伊利诺伊大学厄巴纳 – 香槟分校档案馆馆藏资料

责任编辑：周 菊　　责任校对：张万莹　　封面设计：有品堂　　责任印制：周荣虎

著　　者	陶行知
译　　者	张汉敏　周洪宇
出版发行	东南大学出版社
社　　址	南京四牌楼 2 号　邮编：210096
网　　址	http://www.seupress.com
经　　销	全国各地新华书店
印　　刷	南京艺中印务有限公司
开　　本	700 毫米 × 1000 毫米　1/16
印　　张	16.5
字　　数	220 千
版　　次	2022 年 12 月第 1 版
印　　次	2022 年 12 月第 1 次印刷
书　　号	ISBN 978-7-5766-0361-3
定　　价	68.00 元

（本社图书若有印装质量问题，请直接与营销部调换。电话（传真）：025-83791830）

陶行知

师德师风系列丛书

丛书主编 张策华

南京市属高校"十四五"市级哲学社会科学重点研究基地
"陶行知教育思想及其当代价值研究"资助

丛书序

在学习宣传贯彻党的二十大精神热潮下，南京晓庄学院陶行知研究院学术研究蔚然成风，学陶师陶研陶成果势成穰穰，编著的"陶行知师德师风系列丛书"即将付梓面世，我深感欣慰并致以学术上的祝贺！

师德师风是评价教师队伍素质的第一标准，是广大教师努力成为"四有"好老师的第一要求。习近平总书记在党的二十大报告中指出"育人的根本在于立德""加强师德师风建设，培养高素质教师队伍，弘扬尊师重教社会风尚"。建立起完备的师德师风建设制度体系和有效的师德师风建设长效机制是教育者、研究者、全社会有关方面共同努力的方向。

陶行知是伟大的人民教育家，他是师德师风的典范，有着"爱满天下"的仁爱之心，"捧着一颗心来，不带半根草去"的奉献精神，"为一大事来，做一大事去"的教育情怀。陶行知波澜壮阔的教育生涯中展现出的以理想信念、道德情操、扎实学识、仁爱之心为核心的崇高师德，成为一笔弥足珍贵的精神财富和教育财富。我每次有机会到国内很多地方调研交流时，总要谈及"传承弘扬陶行知教育思想精髓"

话题，学习之余深感陶行知伟大光辉的一生和鞠躬尽瘁的精神令人赞叹。我也曾撰文《大先生陶行知》，宣扬陶行知先生立志、立德、立功、立言，作为"中国近代教育史上当之无愧的大先生"的风采。陶行知先生身体力行、知行合一，体现了其鲜明的师德观，这也是他崇高的人生观、道德观、价值观的集中表现，对新时期加强师德师风建设具有重要的现实意义与借鉴价值。

陶行知老校长创办的南京晓庄学院，是全国知名的教师教育特色鲜明的大学，这里是中国乡村教育运动的试验场，也是陶行知"生活教育"理论的发源地。"晓庄"因行知先生享誉世界，蔡元培、陈鹤琴、赵叔愚等一批我国近代著名教育家曾于此执教。今年恰逢学校建校95周年，95年来，学校传承弘扬陶行知教育思想，形成了"教学做合一"的校训和"教人求真，学做真人"的校风，为社会培养输送了17余万名基础教育师资和各类专门人才，涌现出数百名中小学特级教师、教学名师和教育管理者，被誉为"中小学教师的摇篮"，连续两年在校友会中国应用型师范院校一流专业排名中位列第一。今年9月，学校第三次党代会胜利召开，提出百年晓庄将迈上奋力建设新时代教师教育特色鲜明的高水平大学新征程。在新发展阶段，学校一直在教师教育方面，特别在师德师风领域，传承弘扬陶行知教育思想精髓，努力贡献晓庄力量、晓庄智慧。几个突出方面有：一是2020年江苏省教育厅向南京晓庄学院授牌"江苏师德教育基地"，去年陶行知先生诞辰130周年时，全国第一家师德教育馆在南京晓庄学院开馆，这为师德师风教育研究提供了优良的平台和基础。二是组织召开培养造就新时代"大先生"研讨会，邀请国内外学者嘉宾共同研讨新时代"大先生"的意蕴和成长路径，号召全国教师努力成长为新时代"大先生"。三是今年教师节，学校发布了《教师教育蓝皮书：中国教师教育发展报告（2022）》，其中章节揭示了改革开放以来我国师德师风建设的发展特征，指出了未来我国师德师风建设的努力方向。四是学校总体形成"以陶育人"的师德教育"晓庄模式"，开发了以"拜谒一次陶墓、参观一次陶馆、阅读一本陶著、观看一部陶行知影视剧、聆听一次关于陶行知的学术讲座、抒写一篇学陶师陶心得"为主要内容的系列师德教育课程，形成了以"坚定理想信念、厚植爱国情怀、传承大爱精神、铸造高尚师魂"为价值追求的师德教育模式。未来，学校将持续建设全国师德教育基地，以行知思想为依托打造师德师风研究实践高地。

陶行知研究院是南京晓庄学院设立的一个专门宣传、研究和实践陶行知思想的科研机构，也是中国陶行知研究会秘书处所在地。这次组织编著"陶行知师德师风系列丛书"是在去年"陶行知教育思想新视野研究丛书"基础上，继续深化研究主题、凝练研究方向、汇聚研究队伍的进一步探索，进一步总结梳理了新时代学陶研陶师陶的新经验。丛书包括《陶行知师德师风教育文选》（张济洲、于涛编）、《陶行知：民主之魂，教育之光——〈救国时报〉〈新华日报〉〈解放日报〉刊文选（1936—1946）》（王文岭、徐莹晖编著）、《中国之租借地——陶行知硕士论文（英汉）》（张汉敏、周洪宇译）。丛书以文选的形式，对陶行知及其师德教育思想进行侧写，是学校陶行知研究工作的又一成果，对学校推动教师教育特色化建设起到重要作用。

办好人民满意的教育是时代所盼。南京晓庄学院是一所有着深厚历史底蕴、深切人文情怀、巨大创新潜能的大学，努力建设学术晓庄、人文晓庄、创新晓庄。学校将始终传承弘扬陶行知教育思想精髓，深化陶行知教育思想和师德师风研究，努力做"为学""为人""为事"的"大先生"，必然会驰而不息、开拓创新，抓住强师计划新机遇，拓展与形成富有时代意蕴的教师教育新理念、新经验、新模式，为建设教育强国贡献力量。这是新时代晓庄人义不容辞的责任担当，愿与同仁共勉。

我衷心期盼通过此套丛书，南京晓庄学院的各位专家学者矢志不渝、笃行不怠，在教师教育、陶行知研究等各个方面与国内外专家多联系多交流，不断拓展新视野、开辟新赛道，取得新成果、达到新高度。

张策华

2022 年 12 月 8 日于南京方山

目　录

导读：在民族生死存亡关头筑起"新之长城"

　　　　　　　　　　　　　　张汉敏　周洪宇 / 001

《中国之租借地》　　　　　　　　　　陶文濬

第一章　引言　　　　　　　　　　　　　/ 001

第二章　胶州湾　　　　　　　　　　　　/ 005

第三章　关东　　　　　　　　　　　　　/ 037

第四章　广州湾　　　　　　　　　　　　/ 063

第五章　威海卫　　　　　　　　　　　　/ 069

第六章　九龙（新界）　　　　　　　　　/ 079

第七章　结论　　　　　　　　　　　　　/ 085

附录

　　甲：参考文献　　　　　　　　　　　/ 095

　　乙：汇率换算表　　　　　　　　　　/ 098

Leased Territories in China Wen-Tsing Tao

Ⅰ. INTRODUCTION / 103

Ⅱ. KIAO CHOW / 109

Ⅲ. KWANTUNG / 151

Ⅳ. KWANG CHOW WAN / 187

Ⅴ. WEI HAI WEI / 193

Ⅵ. KOWLOON / 205

Ⅶ. CONCLUSIONS / 213

APPENDIX

A. BIBLIOGRAPHY / 225

B. TABLE OF CURRENCY VALUES / 229

在民族生死存亡关头筑起"新之长城"

——陶行知硕士论文《中国之租借地》导读

Construction of a New Great Wall at the Critical Time for Chinese Nation: Preface to the Chinese Version of *Leased Territories in China*（Tao Xingzhi's M.A. Thesis）

张汉敏　周洪宇

（华中师范大学教育学院，陶行知国际研究中心）

摘要：在一个国力孱弱、政治黑暗的时代，奢谈科技兴国毫无实际意义，这也是陶行知弃医从文的原因。而最终获誉"万世师表"的陶行知不仅在教育领域，而且在哲学、政治学和历史学等人文社科领域都有杰出的成就。反映在陶行知硕士论文《中国之租借地》（*Leased Territories in China*）上，是他昂扬的民族气节、开阔的学术视野和植根于民生而又极为严谨的治学态度与方法，继而折射出的是陶行知一以贯之的爱国主义精神、学术报国的志向和经世致用的大贤风范。当署名陶文濬的作者在论文结语处号召国人构筑"新之长城"时，译者——也是读者——难免血脉偾张，感佩陶行知伟大爱国情怀的同时，也深知陶先生治学理念、方法及作为对当下我国学界的借鉴意义。

关键词：陶行知；《中国之租借地》；爱国主义；学术报国；经世致用；新之长城

Abstract: At the time when the strength of one's motherland was weak and the international political environment was extremely unfavorable, it was of little pragmatic meaning to think about revitalizing the country through scientific and technological achievements. That was why Tao Xingzhi (still Wen-Tsing Tao at that time) should have abandoned medicine for literature. While Tao, who was later honored as the "model of all ages", had made outstanding achievements not only in the field of education, but also in those of philosophy, politics, history and other humanities and social sciences. His high national integrity, broad academic vision, and extremely rigorous academic attitude and methods that had been rooted in people's livelihood were all reflected in his English graduation thesis for an M. A. degree: *Leased Territories in China*. Probing deep into the thesis, we can see Tao's consistent patriotism, academic ambition and Confucian style of service to his country. When the author, who signs himself as Wen-Tsing Tao, calls on the Chinese people to build a new Great Wall at the conclusion of the thesis, the translators, who are readers as well, cannot help feeling inspired. Thus, the translators, while extremely moved by Tao's great patriotic thoughts, are quite clear that Tao's academic conception, methodology, and achievements would be of great referential meaning for the current Chinese academic circles.

Key words: Tao Xingzhi; *Leased Territories in China;* patriotism; academic ambition; Confucian style of serving the country; a New Great Wall

1915年，在美国伊利诺伊大学攻读政治学硕士学位的陶行知（时年仍用名陶文濬）在其毕业论文中写道："然因中国积弱，租借地之法律主权无从确保。"① 在一个国力屡弱、政治黑暗的时代，国家领土尚且难以保存完整、主权也无从确保，奢谈科技兴国毫无实际意义，这也是人们所熟知的陶行知放弃医学专业转向社科人文的主要原因。而最终获誉"万世师表"的陶行知不仅在教育领域，而且在哲学、政治、经济、法律、宗教和历史学等人文社科领域都有涉猎，并且成就斐然，这些在他的这篇英文硕士论文中已有淋漓尽致的体现。细细读来，在《中国之租借地》一文中，陶行知昂扬的民族气节、开阔的学术视野和植根于民生而又极为严谨的治学态度与方法清晰可见，继而折射出的是陶行知一以贯之的爱国主义精神、学术报国的志向和经世济用的大贤风范。

虽然此篇论文撰写时间至今已逾百年，但其选题之新颖、视野之开阔、结构之严谨、资料之丰富、分析之深刻、结论之坚实，仍令人无限感慨与由衷钦佩。本文从小说，堪称研究生毕业论文的最佳样板；望大看，不难从中窥见那个大时代改革先驱者思想演进的心路历程，启发后人沿着前辈探索的道路继续前行，为中华民族的伟大复兴添砖加瓦。

深植于心的民族气节与爱国主义精神

租借地虽非租界，但与租界关系密切，性质类似。清末官员屡屡混淆"租界"、"租地"与"租借地"等概念，至民国初年始有从西方学成归来的中国外交官注意到二者之间的差异，并于1919年的巴黎和会上将"归还租借地"和"归还租界"并列为"希望条件"中的两项。② 陶行知在1915年撰写硕士论文时即已清楚地认识到租借地

---

① 参见陶文中译稿《中国之租借地》"结语"部分。
② 费成康：《中国租界史》，上海社会科学院出版社，1991年，第309—318页。

的特殊性，将租借地（leased territory）清晰地界定为"一国在规定时间内向另一国割让使用权及管理权之领土。租让国在"租借"期间放弃租借地上一应管理权；然约定之"租借"期满，租让国有权收回一应割让之权益及特许权力"。陶文在目录及引言中均明确指出近代中国历史上的五大租借地分别为胶州湾、关东、广州湾、威海卫与九龙（"新界"）；而在第六章中，更是将北九龙（即"新界"）与香港和一度亦为租借地的（南）九龙区分开来。仅此一项，已足见陶行知学术嗅觉之敏锐、学术视野之开阔、学术认知之深刻。

然而，最让读者感佩的还是陶行知的勇气。撰写该硕士论文时，辛亥革命已然爆发，但列强在中国的"势力范围"犹在，长期的半封建半殖民地社会令中国积重难返；北洋军阀政府对外软弱、对内强横，不仅根本不敢触碰列强在华势力，还助纣为虐、极力打压国内反对帝国主义的爱国声音与行动。时年第一次世界大战业已爆发，在美国留学和攻读硕士学位的陶行知若出于对自身安全的考虑只针对美国的非盟友如德国、日本、沙皇俄国等就租借地一事发出批评与抨击之声，也能够为人们所理解。但陶行知全然不畏强权，文中对美国的盟友英法两国一视同仁，甚至在涉及美国的相关事务上也毫无溢美之词，纯粹据实阐述和分析，丝毫不考虑由此可能对论文评阅带来的不利影响。这与过往及现在学术研究中存在的诸多功利现象形成鲜明的对照。

陶文开宗明义，在界定了租借地的概念之后，即简要介绍了租借地的历史和由来，接着指出中国的租借地包括胶州湾、关东、广州湾、威海卫与九龙（"新界"）等总计 5 片、总面积达 2,250 平方英里的土地，然后貌似冷峻而实则痛心疾首、义愤填膺地指出："列强达成租约之手段堪称霸道，租约签订之条件亦极为苛刻。凡此类租约均体现该特殊国际关系历经发展之极致形态"。

陶文第一章"引言"的最后一部分明确指出上述 5 片租借地作为中国的门户、作为军事基地和商贸中心对中国的重要性，"且为列强恶意在中国扩大其势力范围之肇始",因此,"将其使用权及管理权割让予他国其危害可想而知"。在此基础上,陶文明确了"本文意欲探讨及解决之问题":包括"遭强行租借之后",租借地与中国内陆的关系问题;作为商贸中心的重要性问题;作为军事基地的重要性问题;列强借由租借地扩张势力范围的问题;各租借地的相互关系和重要性地位问题等。当然,此处陶文提出的最后两个问题应该是论文作者所要探讨的终极问题,那就是租借地对中国主权的影响问题和"中国应如何应对列强之蛮横行径"的问题。

陶文接下来在第二至六章中分别对胶州湾、关东、广州湾、威海卫和九龙("新界")五个租借地的名称、位置、面积、自然与人文环境、军事基地建设与军用价值、贸易地位与经贸发展、各租借地(主要是借由铁路)与中国内陆乃至租借国的关联、列强借由租借地扩张势力范围的情况以及租借地对于租借国的影响与意义等加以介绍、分析和论述。当然,每一章中对于租借地的由来或者说"租借"的过程都有详细的介绍以及基于确凿而丰富史料之上的论证,另外加上胶州湾从德国、关东从俄国落入日本人手中的介绍与论证,陶文就租借地一事对帝国主义列强强行霸占中国土地、侵犯中国主权、扩张在华势力范围并进而意欲瓜分中国的丑恶嘴脸及殖民行径进行了无情的揭露与讽刺。

帝国主义对外殖民的过程中,往往打着促进文明进程、播撒上帝福音的旗号,但其真实的目的无外乎拓展"帝国的利益"。陶文第二章提及德国总理冯·布洛埃在国会的讲话:"中国已然四分五裂,原因与吾等毫不相干。"由此可见德意志帝国对于中国人的疾苦并不关心。紧接着冯·布洛埃的发言"但无论如何,吾等断不可空手而归"则清楚地暴露了德意志帝国的狼子野心。最终德国借由所谓"巨野惨案"发兵胶州湾并占领了这一地区。在发兵前德国政府给驻华公使冯·海靖的政府电令"索取极致之赔偿",且"无轻言满意之条件"

可谓无耻之极,却也是本性毕露。陶文对发兵前德皇兄弟之间对话的引用更是充分暴露了德意志帝国高层的尔虞我诈、惺惺作态以及对强权的渴望与倚仗,什么促进德国商贸"平稳繁荣发展"、什么保护德国海外侨民正当权益,统统不如"我辈新近统一而崛起之德意志帝国跨洋殖民目标"重要,亨利王子对此理解深刻,将它看作"吾皇之福音",并且誓言"无论得遇倾听与否,吾当竭尽全力,铭刻此福音于吾达到之每一地方"。陶文将"此番基尔城堡对话"视作是"文明戏之对白","如非亵渎上帝,亦属不可理喻,委实滑稽可笑"。可见,在帝国主义者那里,文明不过是一场游戏,强权才是"真理",租借地正是强权政治的产物。

沙俄对于旅大港的"租借"与德国强占胶州湾如出一辙。陶文指出:"《中俄密约》加速了德国占领胶州湾;反之,德国租借胶州湾亦加速沙俄对旅顺口及大连湾地区之操控"。"1898年3月6日,中德双方签订《胶澳租借条约》;3月7日,俄方以与德方享有平等权利为借口,大胆提出长期以来之图谋:租借旅顺口和大连湾……于3月27日签署租借条约"。不只是强占租借地的过程类似,沙俄与清政府签订的"租赁"条约也和德国与清政府签订的《胶澳租界条约》基本一致。更为荒诞的是,日俄战争之后,日本竟然胁迫清政府签订条约,"清政府同意沙俄根据条约……向日本进行一切权益之转移及委托"。

德国强占胶州湾是出于对"巨野惨案"的补偿和"保护德国侨民的需要",俄国侵占旅大港则是要求"与德方享有平等权利",而日本接手关东竟直接强迫清政府"转让"权益!在一个国际政治环境异常黑暗的时代,所谓"国际公法"中又焉有正义与公理?国际事务的处理奉行的不过是谁的枪杆子硬谁有理的原则。所以日俄战争的胜利方日本"理所当然地"叫沙俄"转让"并迫使清政府同意"转让"了关东租借地!法国人"租借"广州湾与清政府签订了与《胶澳租界条约》基本一致的条约,但是,"五个海军基地中,广州湾最无军事价值"。

要知道,"列强主要出于军事目的向弱小国家租借的大片战略要地"①才是租借地,那法国人"租借"广州湾即便依从当时的国际政治逻辑也依然欠缺合理性!这样一来,"英国以保护自身在华商业利益不受俄国侵占关东及德国占领胶州湾影响为由,强行租借威海卫"似乎要"合情合理"得多了。但到了1914年11月,"关东及胶州湾相继落入与英国有同盟关系之日本之手","英国已不需要威海卫为其商船之保障",英国理当归还威海卫,然而事实远非如此。陶文接下来对英日两个岛国的对比,表面上是分析两国"同样之需求,同样之供给",实际上却是要揭示两国"同样之野心及争夺目标",揭露英帝国主义和日本帝国主义乃至所有帝国主义国家侵略扩张的本性。至于英国"租借"北九龙("新界"),概因"'新界'既是香港之腹地,亦为香港之屏障"。英国人对"新界"予取予夺,是因为他们早已把香港当成了英国的固有领土、把香港周围当成了英国的"势力范围",这种鸠占鹊巢的霸道行径,也只有惯于侵略扩张的帝国主义列强才会认为理所当然。

待到第七章"结语""五个租借地之对比"一节中,陶文对五个租借地的租借方式也做了一番总结,三言两语间给帝国主义列强作了一幅讽刺漫画。这一次陶文再无掩饰,称"德国首开武力强占胶州湾之先河,列强以保障本国在华利益为借口,纷起效仿",又称德国人"不加掩饰",而俄罗斯人和法国人则"口蜜腹剑"。至于"一向彬彬有礼"的英国人,"初则助中国抵制俄罗斯,后则改弦更张,加入掠夺者行列";"租借威海卫情有可原……然其坚持租借九龙之意令人费解"。陶文引用某些人的说法,"租赁九龙以卫香港",下一句即切中要害:"然卫戍何许人也?"陶文中,外表文质彬彬、实则张牙舞爪的英帝国主义者之丑恶嘴脸跃然纸上。到了这一段的最后一句,陶文以深得

---

① 费成康:《中国租借史》,上海社会科学院出版社,1991,第309页。

英式幽默的语言写道："当然，英国人依然可以保护远东和平为由替自身辩护。"当然，这实在是有贼喊捉贼的意味！

当然，租借方式只是形式问题，陶文所要探讨的核心问题是租借地的主权之争。在第七章"结语"第二节"对中国领土主权之法律效力"中，陶文仍貌似冷峻、实则痛心疾首地指出中国领土上的租借地虽存在差异，但在"租赁条约"方面都有类似之处：租期内中国在租借地上不得行使管理权；中国军舰需征得租借国许可方能在租借地港口停靠；租借国始终有权在租借地上建造军事防御工事；"除威海卫外，列强均有依托租借地扩张势力范围之机会"。事实上，这种所谓"租赁条约"给予了租借地如租界一般"国中之国"的地位，让"租让国"中国在租借期满前丧失了租借地的主权。

对于这种丧权辱国的"租赁条约"，陶文首先从法理上论证了它们的不合理性。简而言之，在一贯尊崇私有制的西方，租让方始终拥有土地及房产的主权，即便是永久出租，西方亦有案例裁定出租人仍是地产之主人。由此，陶文做出合理推论："既如此，是否可以说，中国对关东、胶州湾、威海卫、九龙新界及广州湾仍然拥有主权，而日本、英国及法国仅能在租期内行使其享有之权利？"紧接着，陶文区分了"法律主权"和"事实主权"两个概念，论证了就法律主权而言，"中国仅授予租借国租借地之行政管理权，仅转让管理权……依照国际公法，中国有权根据本国法律规定享有租借地之租赁者一应权利"。但是，法理虽如此，"就实际情况来看，中国之法律主权已遭严重伤害"。陶文以各国均在租借地上修筑军事及防御工事为例说明因为租借地的存在，中国不仅用自己的土地为他国提供战场，而且动辄被列强裹挟加入他国的战争，根本无法保持中立，遑论维护"远东"乃至国际和平。陶文言下之意因而呼之欲出：这是对法律的挑战，是对国际公法的挑衅，是对"远东"乃至国际和平的威胁。陶文借用劳伦斯的观点批驳了一切为此种"租赁"方式所做的辩护，断言"中国真正租让者不惟领土，更有主权"。

当此危局，中国应该何去何从？历史上从来都不乏投降派，所以当时"永久租让"说以及寻求列强"看家护院"说甚嚣尘上。然而，历史从来只会让不畏强权、不惧牺牲、勇于反抗外来侵略的民族英雄名垂千古、永载史册！陶行知此时展示的正是他昂扬的民族气节和坚定的爱国主义立场。他向"诸君"发出了振聋发聩的警告："此五处租借地乃中国之重要门户，须得中国人自己守护"。事实上，早在第三章《关东》的结尾处，陶文即借用米勒德先生的话明确指出："面对列强，中国惟有奋发图强，才有可能维持远东国际势力均衡，依靠自己，解决纠纷"。自家的门户自家看守，本国的事情本国解决。陶文立场坚定、态度坚决、铿锵有力、掷地有声："中国应保持其领土及主权完整，收复租借地。恢复中国在租借地之主权乃吾辈一代人之责任……中国必须明白，世界也必须清楚，中国有数百万平方英里土地可供开放，却不允许一寸土地被占领。"当然，陶文也承认"中国积弱"，所以陶文才借举世闻名的"万里长城"（此处应指两千年前的秦长城）喻指中华民族抵御外族入侵的崇高气节和伟大传统，呼吁当此生死存亡关头，国人应凝聚"新之长城"：

此一"新之长城"不再以巨石及砖块筑成，而是以四万万鲜活之肉体及灵魂，协力同心，矢志凝聚。此一"新之长城"对于收复河山必不可少；对于拱卫今后之新中国不可或缺；对于防止国际冲突、维护远东地区之国际和平亦不可少。

也许今天的国人认为这种"新之长城"及其精神的提法毫无新意，但回到陶文撰写的那个帝国主义在中国横行的时代，陶文立言之新颖、立意之高远、立论之雄奇真可谓高山仰止、震古烁今。有人曾撰文提及陶行知思想与马克思主义学说的关联，笔者（译者）虽烂熟陶行知生平与思想，但囿于1915年前马克思主义学说在中国少有传播，不敢妄言；但笔者笃定陶文提到的"新之长城"和"新中国"的理念对于后来中国的马克思主义者和共产党人都影响深远，陶先生深入骨髓的民族气节和爱国精神应该是他后来作为民主人士深受中国共产党人——包括毛主席和周总理——推崇的主要原因。此时的陶行知虽年少而志存高远、因青春而热血澎湃，他尚不具备后来那个成熟教育家的老练，却有着青年学者不加掩饰的爱国激情。这样的陶行知，也许可以在他后来的文章、演讲、授课和著作中不断被感知，却很难再像在这篇硕士毕业论文中如此一览无余、清晰可见。

开阔的学术视野与扎实的学术功底

虽然陶行知深知在政治黑暗、国力孱弱的时代，悬壶也难以济世，但他显然受到了前朝洋务运动的影响，毕竟陶行知之所以能去美国留学攻读硕士研究生是与洋务运动首创的赴西洋留学之风密切相关的。陶行知也认同"师夷长技以制夷"的思想，所以，即便是对列强强行"租借"中国领土、为本国利益发展租借地并扩张在华势力范围的行径深恶痛绝，但对于列强在租借地上大兴教育并客观上帮助中国人提高教育水平、拓宽视野的措施仍会客观地给予肯定。譬如，对于德国人在青岛大兴教育，陶文一方面尖锐地指出德国政府的目的无外乎于培养德国文化氛围，加速青岛乃至胶州湾的"德国化进程"，另一方面也承认，"当然，不容否认，一些中国青年学子也在这些德式学校获得科学启蒙，激发了科研灵感"。显然，陶行知认同全民素质的提高对爱国救亡的积极意义，这是他个人学术报国志向的一种社会化投影，也是他日后积极从事"生活教育"实践及其"教学做合一"思想的认知基础。

陶行知的学术报国志向在他的硕士毕业论文中主要体现在两个方面：一是他开阔的学术视野，一是他扎实的学术功底。随手翻阅一下陶文，就会发现陶文所涉猎的学科门类多达十余种，涵盖了历史、政治、法律、军事、经济、外语外事、教育、金融、铁路交通、宗教、地理、邮政、农林业等方面。陶行知勤奋好学、博闻强记，在国内教会大学金陵大学学习时，对哲学、伦理学、史学、文学、政治学、法律、社会学、教育学、宗教学等均有涉猎，并在其获得校长包文等教授交口称誉的本科毕业论文《共和精义》中有充分体现。1913年，陶行知受时任金陵大学教授的詹克先生以及在南京布道的著名美国传教士演说家艾迪等人的影响，一度信奉基督教，对基督教教义中平等、博爱、牺牲、奉献的精神产生浓厚兴趣。他留学美国之后，在伊利诺伊大学主修政治学，故其对各租借地的行政管理构成及管理模式均感兴趣并有精准的介绍，这也就不足为奇。前文提及陶文对西洋私法及各类"国际公法"等法律、法理的透彻了解，则已然超出了陶行知主修科目的内容，依照今人的认知，这应该属于"辅修"的范畴。再看看陶行知对外语外事、经济学、政治学、宗教学和历史学等学科知识和研究方法驾轻就熟的运用，我们就不得不钦佩陶先生的学贯中西、通晓古今、多才多艺了。

陶文论及的五个租借地牵涉当时的德、俄、日、法、英五个帝国主义国家，相应地牵涉德、俄、日、法、英五种外文资料的阅读与运用。陶行知无疑是语言奇才，自幼就在家乡歙县教会学校崇一学堂学习英语和西方科学文化，后来在教会大学金陵大学攻读，经常运用英语写作与翻译，有多篇英文传记和文章译作发表。英文演讲曾获得全校第一名，而且据称也擅法语，并曾参加学校法语比赛。后陶行知赴美留学，硕士论文以英文写就，他对英文的熟练运用使得论文容易被理解和接受；不仅如此，而且他对原本属于译文的英文资料的选用也让我们感叹他不同凡响的语言感知力。譬如他选用赖因施《世界公法》对德国总理冯·布洛埃国会讲话的译文"The devil takes the hindmost"可谓一语双关乃至三关：既可指列强如群魔，争先恐后要挤上来中国涂炭生灵的列车；也可指人不为己天诛地灭，德国"害怕中国分裂"并非为中国计，而只是为了"帝国的利益"而已；还可以指德国要抓住最后的机会，要后来者居上！就翻译而言，双关语不少属于"不可译"之列，至于三关语译者更无语义译无疏漏的奢望。由于第三种意味中布洛埃在自鸣得意的同时，不小心暴露了德殖民主义者堪比魔鬼的丑恶本性，再结合上下文，笔者（译者）将该句译为"来得早，不如来得巧"，勉强呈现陶文的部分意蕴，至于不能尽言之处，就只能归结为"翻译是遗憾的艺术了"。陶文整体的英文写作水准也属上乘，不少大学英文教授直言"不可思议"，而我等英文水平"半瓶醋"之辈也只有望洋兴叹、叹为观止了。

  陶文大多数时候采用了英文翻译材料来处理其他外语语种的史料和信息，但有时论文作者也自己亲自阅读原文，并将相应的内容和术语翻译成英文。例如，日文中"旅顺"二字采用了"当用汉字"，与中文（繁体字）写法相同，但发音有异，陶文对此作了准确的标注：Liojun。此举究竟只是论文作者无意中透漏的对于日文的熟悉，还是暗讽日本军国主义者东施效颦、欠缺文化底蕴，笔者无从知悉，但笔者确实在陶文中看到了作者对日本文化的熟悉。例如，陶文根据《日本帝国法令》（全日文）得知"关东政府及其下属机关之最高首脑为关东省省长，由日本驻军中拥有中将或大将衔之最高司令长官担任"。日军中没有上将衔，所谓大将即为上将，故而陶文的翻译非常准确，即为"Lieutenant-General or Full-General"。只是初译时，译者未能虑及日本军衔制的特点，而是照英文直译为"中将或上将"，差点酿成笑谈；所幸审阅时及时发现了问题，避免了笑料的留存。有鉴于此，译者重新校订了译文对所有专有名词的翻译，像德国海军侵占胶州湾的强盗头子"von Diedrichs"就不再依音译翻作"冯·海德里希将军"，而是依习惯译作"棣德利将军"，三艘军舰名称"the Kaiser, Prinzess Wilhem, and Commorant"也依照德文及惯例翻译为"恺撒号、威廉王妃号和鸬鹚号"，而不是依照英文译为"恺撒号、威廉公主号和便民号"。陶文在整体的学术英语之中，不时也掺杂一些口语用法，平易而不失典雅，与这一时期陶行知的中文行文风格相得益彰，因此，译者也尝试以文白夹杂的语言再现陶文的风格。必须声明：如有出彩处，必是陶文精妙；若遇不当及晦涩处，全因译者才学疏漏。

陶文涉及经济学和金融贸易方面的内容有三个特点：重数据、重比对、重分析。陶文惯用数据"说话"，通篇可见各色数据，单为论证胶州湾地理位置的重要性，陶文就采用了8个数据。全文正文五章中数据表格最少的是第四章《广州湾》，表格数为零，但并不是说这一章数据全无（例如，"1912年，广州湾进出口贸易额约8,412,875越币，合3,600,000美元。"）；数据表格最多的是第三章《关东》，有大小表格共10个，其次是第二章《胶州湾》，有大小表格共9个。各色数据以及大大小小的表格使陶文充满了科学论文的色彩，极具西方科研论文重理据的特点。陶文重比对，论及"胶州湾之勃兴及烟台港之没落""在出口领域，胶州湾港口已然完全取代烟台港""大连为近代中国发展最快之口岸""对比下表中日美进口额""其间满洲日本人口数变化""大连及旅顺港中日人口对比"……，陶文都是以数据表格加以比对，以客观数据呈现，让观点不言自明。陶文更重分析，因为有时候数据是死的，人却是活的。例如，对于德国在胶州湾的"巨大投入"和所谓贡献，陶文适时加以分析："开支巨大证明该地区发展繁荣，而财政收入同步增长则表明胶州湾正逐步发展成为自给自足之地。胶州湾很有可能如香港一般，每年财政收支相抵且有盈余。"在谈及1911年关东租借地上超过四分之三的进出口贸易为日本人掌控，陶文即刻做出分析："的确，相对廉价之劳动力、更为低廉之生产成本以及更低廉之运输成本有利于日本进口贸易。"陶文的分析每每切中要害、鞭辟入里、立言新颖、令人信服，极大地提升了论文的创新价值。

涉及历史领域，陶文既有传统历史学研究的特点，也有近似于当今"新历史主义"理论的理念和方法。前者在论文开篇对"租借地"一事历史由来的"考据学"研究中就有淋漓尽致的体现，对"临租"、"永租"和"割让"等案例的援引充分反映了论文作者认真、严谨的学术作风。后者则在陶文对某些"逸闻趣事"和生活细节的引用和论述中有所反映。前文对德皇兄弟基尔城堡的"戏剧性对白"已有介绍,像这种从"文学性"文本中寻找"历史真相"的做法完全符合新历史主义颠覆宏大叙事,注重小写的个体叙事的主张。[①] 另外,对于沙俄对日俄战争的备战,陶文采用了俄罗斯在满洲 8 家面粉产的日产量表加以佐证,笔者在翻译过程中对每一个制粉厂的名字都反复斟酌、认真求证[②],就因为陶文貌似小题大做,但若想到"兵马未动粮草先行"的道理,陶文实可谓旁征博引,且妙趣横生。这种关注细节、关注民生的草根学者作风陶行知一直带入了他后来享誉全国、影响深远的"生活教育"之中。

经世致用的大贤风范

陶行知爱国,但不排外;陶行知有昂扬的民族气节,但他从来不是一个狭隘的民族沙文主义者;陶行知渴望收回所有被"租借"的土地,恢复中国领土主权完整,但他从来就不赞同"闭关锁国",并且深知落后就要挨打的道理;陶行知也渴望能维护中国的和平,但他清楚国家和平和区域和平的关系,明白现代化进程中世界各国的紧密关联。陶行知的硕士毕业论文充分证明,他从来都不是拘泥于死理的腐儒,而始终是经世致用的大才。

陶文自始至终显示了对帝国主义假借"租借"之名,侵占中国领土、侵犯中国主权的愤怒。对殖民主义者的无耻言行,陶文时有言明,时有讥讽,时有无情的鞭挞。以陶行知对基督教的了解,自然知道"福

---

① 参见 H. Aram Veeser, The New Historicism (New York: Routledge, 1989).
② 其中的"诺瓦尔斯基制粉厂"原本译作"诺瓦拉斯基制粉厂",在咨询了俄文专家后才改用这一名称。

音"来自何人，四位先知不过是上帝的信使；那么摘录德皇兄弟的对话，强调亨利王子一心要传播属于德皇的福音，然后指责亨利"亵渎上帝"。"渎神"在宗教世界里从来都是异常严重的指控；陶文对宗教知识的灵活运用轻易就揭示了德皇兄弟的丑恶面目，远比跳脚骂街来得儒雅，关键是更容易引起西方读者的共鸣。无论对殖民行径怎样气愤、怎样痛恨，陶文从不吝啬对租借地上外国人"作为"和"贡献"的肯定，如在第二章《胶州湾》"德国人在胶州湾之其他作为"一节中，陶文就详细开列了德国人在"煤矿开采""拓荒与耕种""邮局""咨政""传教""教育"和"土地问题"等方面对胶州湾所做的"贡献"。这种情况下，陶文很少直接做出分析与评判，除了不动声色地揭露殖民主义者贪婪与侵略的本质外（如在"土地问题"这一小节中所做的那样），陶文更多的是引用外国人自己的评论来揭示殖民者名义上促进地方发展、促进中国发展，实质上永远都是追逐自身利益的阴险本性。譬如，为了证明德国传教士不仅要为上帝服务，同样也在为"帝国"服务，陶文就引用了米尔布的话语"吾等理当相信签订殖民地条约将有利德意志帝国之发展"；为了说明德国人在租借地大兴教育的真实目的是推广德语以有利于"德国化"的进程，陶文引用梅尔伯特的话说，"世界各国人民都需要接受更好之教育，尤其需要学好德语"。陶行知的学问都被用来治事、救世，他的确是朝着经世致用的方向努力着。

陶文善用"以子之矛攻子之盾"的方法。不说在德国侵占胶州湾事件上陶文不断昭示德国后来的要求与条约条款与早先的声明相悖之处，不说英国"租借"威海卫理由的荒谬，单说陶文在"门户开放"政策上的态度也可以看出其擅长借力打力的特点。"门户开放"政策的初衷不是"促进宗教、艺术及商业交流"嘛，那就要保持中国的领土与主权完整，令中国可以以独立自主的身份与各国交流。

虽然处于乱世之中，虽然中国积弱，但陶文仍不失泱泱中华的气度。陶文直言：

恢复对租借地行使主权并不意味着排外。中国必须对所有国家展现宽容、公正及友好，追求国家主权及领土完整并维护世界和平。中国必须认识到自身对人类之义务。中国应以维护全人类，尤其是维护中国之利益为目标及国策方为惟一正确之选。

对于中国以及列强应该如何看待租借地和最终解决租借地的问题，陶文也是利用西方的法律、国际事务、国际安全认知循循善诱地告诫各方：

一国侵犯另一国，为国家犯罪行为；然若一国任由列强围猎，则属国际犯罪行为。此一国家行为不仅危及其自身生存安全，亦将成为国际冲突之导火索。听凭外国人看守中国之门户，任由中国处于外族入侵及列强贪婪掠夺之下，会对中国及世界之和平与福祉构成威胁。为中国计，亦为全世界计，中国人有责任及使命收回租借之领土。

译完陶文，又几经修改、订正，竟然第一次发现翻译可以是如此愉快的学习过程，不仅能够学习语言，还可以学思想、学精神、学治学、学做人，虽然"学陶师陶"无法"出世便是破蒙"，但一旦开启，便是我们终其一生的学业和志业。

附记：译者张汉敏系华中师范大学教育学院博士研究生，陶行知国际研究中心研究员。周洪宇系华中师范大学教育学院教授、博士生导师，陶行知国际研究中心主任。陶行知先生英文硕士论文的发现者和提供者为宁波大学教师教育学院的刘训华教授。在此谨向刘训华教授致以衷心感谢！

陶

中国之租借地

政治学

文学硕士

1915

伊利诺伊大学图书馆

中国之租借地

陶文濬（金陵大学文学学士，1914）

申请学位　文学硕士
学科专业　政治科学
院　　系　研究生院
学　　校　伊利诺伊大学
提交日期　1915年6月5日

兹郑重声明由我指导之硕士论文

作　者　　陶文濬

题　目　　中国之租借地

完全符合 **文学硕士** 毕业论文之要求

指导教师　詹姆士·厄尔·罗素

系 主 任　W.G.詹姆士

以下为申请博士学位所需，申请硕士学位无此项要求。

目　录

第一章　引言　　　　　　　　　/ 001
第二章　胶州湾　　　　　　　　/ 005
第三章　关东　　　　　　　　　/ 037
第四章　广州湾　　　　　　　　/ 063
第五章　威海卫　　　　　　　　/ 069
第六章　九龙（新界）　　　　　/ 079
第七章　结论　　　　　　　　　/ 085

附录甲：参考文献　　　　　　　/ 093
附录乙：汇率换算表　　　　　　/ 099

第一章

引言

第一章 引言

"租借地"者,为一国在规定时间内向另一国割让使用权①及管理权②之领土。租让国在"租借"期间放弃租借地上一应管理权;然约定之"租借"期满,租让国有权收回一应割让之权益及特许权力。

"租借"之方式并非源于中国。其实,此种将国家领土所有权及行政管理权分离之概念并不新颖,《罗马法》中对此早有详尽记载,然而此种记载直至近期才为人发现。中世纪时期,"租借"最初系以抵押方式出现。1294年,英格兰国王爱德华一世允许法国国王腓力四世派遣驻军驻扎加斯科涅,以解决两国之间长期以来之领土纠纷。③ 1803年,瑞典答应以1,258,000泰勒租金将维斯玛尔镇租借给德国梅克伦堡-什未林大公国,租期100年;租借期满,瑞典有权收回维斯玛尔镇,条件是以3%之年利率返还租金。④ 同样还有桑给巴尔苏丹于1888年和1890年分别"租借"给英国东非公司之"大陆自治领地",租期50年,1891年延长至"永租"。⑤ 类似案例还包括1894年5月12日英国和刚果签订之条约,据此条约,刚果国王承认1890年7月1日英德条约中规定之英国在刚果之势力范围,同时允诺大不列颠可从该势力范围中划分出部分领土作为租借地;而在刚果国王在位期间,该领土尚且包括法绍达镇,国王逊位之后租借地之范围才有所缩小。⑥ 此类案例形象诠释了所谓"租借地"之起源与发展。但是,直到"租借法则"强加至中国头上,我们才发现租借地是如此关系重大、影响深远,值得我们认真研究。

仅1898年一年间,中国就有总面积达2,250平方英里之5片领土

---

① 科贝特,《国际法重要案例》,第一章,第110页。
② 佩林贾凯,《领土临时移交》,第106页。
③ 劳伦斯,《国际公法原理》,第175页。
④ 奥本海,《国际公法》,第一卷,第221页。
⑤ 韦斯特莱克,《国际公法》,第一部分,第135页。
⑥ 同上,第一部分,第132、136页。"零租金租借及无时限征用皆不属于真正意味之租借,仅视同转让。"引自《国际公法学报》。

"租借"给了外国,其中包括租借给德国之山东胶州湾①、租借给俄国之旅大港②、租借给英国之威海卫及九龙,以及租借给法国之广州湾。列强达成租约之手段堪称霸道,租约签订之条件亦极为苛刻。凡此类租约均体现该特殊国际关系历经发展之极致形态。

这五个租借地作为中国之门户,既为军事要塞亦为商贸中心,且为列强恶意在中国扩大其势力范围之肇始。各租借地于中国之地位皆举足轻重,而将其使用权及管理权割让予他国其危害可想而知。凡此门户之地遭强行租借之后,它们与中国内陆之关系如何?作为中国之商贸中心,其重要性又如何?作为中国之海军基地,其重要性几何?列强又是如何借此进一步扩大自身之势力范围?哪个租借地更重要?倘从法律层面看,此5处租借地之割让对中国主权形成何种之影响?中国应如何应对列强之蛮横行径?凡此种种皆为本文意欲探讨及解决之问题。

---

① 1914年被日本攻占。
② 1905年转让给日本。

第二章

胶州湾

第二章　胶州湾

胶州湾乃德国在中国山东沿海地区攫取之租借地，总面积高达193平方英里，尚且不含200平方英里之海湾及2,500平方英里之中立区。1898年3月6日，中国将胶州湾租借给德国；自此直至1914年11月6日，德国一直在胶州湾行使行政管理权。第一次世界大战爆发后，日本于1914年11月占领胶州湾。

从其所处地理位置来看，胶州湾之重要性仅次于关东。胶州湾距离上海390英里，距离威海卫仅270英里，距离天津334英里，距离旅顺港300英里。① 从胶州湾到北里湾仅需7小时，到达白河（天津河）也只需25小时，到达仁川济物浦只需23小时、横渡朝鲜海峡直达日本中部海域也不过30小时。② 因其地理位置之特殊性，德国旅行家、地理学家冯·里希特霍芬强烈建议德国政府将山东省作为在中国拓展势力范围首选省份，而将胶州湾视作是绝佳据点。③ 亦即此冯·里希特霍芬，还从地质学角度论及山东之优势——该省拥有丰富矿物资源，而胶州湾之优势则在于拥有足够支撑制霸中国北部海域之煤炭供应。④ 胶州湾因其地理位置重要早就享有中国第二旅顺港之美誉；而就其经济增长之迅速程度而言，胶州湾则有可能成长为中国之旧金山。⑤ 正是因为胶州湾此种显而易见之地理优势，哈丁先生曾郑重指出："在环绕青岛之群山之中，有一把通往未知帝国之钥匙"。⑥ 就文化心理而言，山东乃中国儒家文化发源地，租借胶州湾乃德国入侵中国标志性一步，亦为列强入侵中国内陆之肇端。因此，1898年被称为中国"败亡之年"，概因胶州湾成为租借地此一事件所致。故而但凡提及胶州湾及其他租借地，中国人难免悲愤难鸣，正如一提到【割让给德

---

① 《中国年鉴》，1914年，第5页。
② 切拉达姆，《殖民地与德国殖民地》，第129页。
③ 《见地》，1914年11月刊，第579页。
④ 《殖民地》，1898年1月6日。
⑤ 同③。
⑥ 同③，第575页。

国的——译者注】阿尔萨斯-洛林地区法国人就不免心头刺痛一般。

加速殖民进程：德国之狼子野心

19世纪中期，对欧洲，特别是对德国而言，殖民地价值并不大。德国首相俾斯麦曾回忆说，当时德国国力强盛，维持现状即可，无意也无需对外扩张。直至19世纪最后二十年完成统一大业之后，为发展经济和稳定政治局势，德国才开始向弱小国家租借战略要地，扩张其势力范围。①

造成德国加速殖民进程之原因为人口膨胀及大量移民涌出。德国狂热沙文主义者崔托奇克之演讲中对此予以验证：他曾哀叹德意志帝国每年竟有25万人流往境外。崔托奇克希望在德国难以立足之国民去到国外以后依然能够生活在德国政府管理之下；他认为德国离散人口可以去往德国殖民地，于是帝国富余劳动力依然可为帝国资产负债表储值。因此，对于一个人口膨胀之国家而言，扩张殖民地自是较好之选择。②

此外，国外优质商品大量流入亦激发了德国青年之爱国热情，使他们纷纷外出找寻能生产出同样品质商品之土地。德国工业化及商业化程度一年高过一年，远超英国以外其他西方国家；当时英德食物供给主要依靠进口，而工业原材料大部分也无法由本国提供。德国经济发展之特殊性也促使其成为一个殖民主义国家。③

凡此种种，德国政府体会到殖民扩张之重要性，首相俾斯麦也一

---

① 赖因施，《殖民政府》，第10页。
② 《19世纪》，1914年11月刊，第959页。
③ 科洪，《掌控太平洋》，第405页。

第二章　胶州湾

改初衷、呼吁国会支持个人对外殖民扩张。1880年，德意志帝国境内对殖民扩张之态度亦发生根本性转变，人们纷纷改弦更张；各地民众或发出"太迟了"之呐喊，或牢骚满腹、不断抱怨帝国先前之消极态度，亦有好战分子煽动对外发起战争。由于俾斯麦所采取之大胆而果断的政治措施以及帝国境内民众及企业之积极响应，至1884年德国已成功占领6个殖民地，分别为多哥兰、南非、喀麦隆【德属喀麦隆，今喀麦隆的一部分——译者注】、恺撒·威廉兰、俾斯麦群岛以及德属东非。此后，德国再难轻易占领其他殖民地。彼时德国殖民地除南非位于亚热带气候区，其他均处于热带气候区内。野心勃勃之德国焉能满足于"受到限制之帝国"及条件有限之殖民地？决定德意志帝国能否实现其"一统世界"之野心关键在于能否在温带地区占领殖民地。1860年，英法联军入侵中国，暴露清政府之软弱无能；1894年中日甲午战争爆发，中华民族更是陷入空前之民族危机。然，于德国人而言，此时之中国恰为德国实现其殖民扩张之野心带来绝佳机会。

势力均衡论

西方列强纷纷在远东扩张势力范围是导致德国意图在中国扩张殖民地之重要原因。必须承认，在强租胶州湾之前，德国是列强中唯一对中国政治事务不具决定性影响之国家。德国总理冯·布洛埃曾在德国国会大厦演讲中讲道："不容否认，倘若吾辈无法在远东建立军事基地，吾等就无法扩张帝国在远东之势力范围。吾辈需要一个进入中国市场之门户，就像东京【法属印度支那联邦之一——译者注】之于法国、香港之于英国、法国北部之于德国一样……吾辈应该【在远东】获取和其他国家一样之权益。倘无自身之领地，则德国之智慧、技术和经济实力均无从体现；此即如为他家花园施肥，断然无法结出属于自家之果实。吾辈要在中国获得一个海军前哨站之要求必须加以实现。"① 德国认为胶州湾正是适合他们实施远东侵略计划之军事基地。

动因二：担心中国分裂

德国加速入侵中国另一个原因较为奇怪：德国害怕中国分裂，故而意欲迅速在中国站稳脚跟以便适时攫取利益。德国总理冯·布洛埃在国会讲话中提道："中国已然四分五裂，原因与吾等毫不相干。但无论如何，吾等断不可空手而归。游客虽无权要求列车何时发车，但须确保发车时自己已然登车。来得早，不如来得巧！"② 德国此等入侵战略貌似极具威胁，甚至可能助其长期占领中国之土地，但列强之间嫉妒之心理、我中华民族团结之意志最终令德国之企图未能得逞。而对德国人而言，霸占胶州湾是其入侵必由途径。自此，德国铺开了其入侵中国之战略规划。

霸占胶州湾之前奏

德国关于胶州湾之第一份记录源自1861年冯·李希霍芬之中国之行期间。但是，正如安德烈·切拉达姆先生所言，直至1891年，侵占胶州湾之秘密计划才为德国所接受。③ 1894年中日甲午战争期间，数国战舰不时短暂停靠胶州湾，令胶州湾地理优势扬名列强，德俄尤甚。至此，德国对胶州湾兴趣愈发浓厚，德国政界对胶州湾势在必得。德国在与法俄合力迫使日本将辽东半岛归还清政府之过程中起到了主要作用，其目的恰是为了索取赔偿，而德国心仪之选正是胶州湾。李

---

① 《日本每周邮报》，1898年3月26日。冯·勃兰特亦曾发表类似且更为详尽之言论，参见《论坛》，第25期，第257—266页。
② 赖因施，《世界政治》，第164页。
③ 德国的远东战略，参见《国中之国》，第31卷，第737页。

鸿章在出使德国时，德国政府表示德国愿意租借或者购买经两国协商之中国任一领土，实指山东胶州湾。① 1896 年，《中俄密约》出台，进一步加速德国占领胶州湾之进程。②《密约》之真实内容无从考据，据称其中第九条提到中国同意将胶州湾租借给沙俄，允许沙俄在此驻扎空军或海军，租期为 15 年；但为避免引起其他列强不满，要求沙俄不可立刻派兵进驻胶州湾。因《密约》内容外泄，德国人大怒。《青岛及周边指南》上记载，1897 年 1 月 8 日，应迪德里克斯要求，柏林政府派遣一名港口建筑和工程专家赴中国考察，之后该专家提交了一份中国考察报告，在德国国内获得积极反响。随即德国政府向中国政府提出租借胶州湾之要求，遭到中国政府拒绝。但德国人并未就此放弃侵占胶州湾之野心，一方面是因为德国人有在中国建立殖民地之强烈愿望，另一方面是因为冯·李希霍芬等人非常看好胶州湾。德国人想要实现这个愿望，唯一办法就是找个借口，当然，此亦仅为时间问题而已。

德国占领胶州湾

1897 年 11 月 1 日，两名德国传教士尼尔和齐格勒在山东省曹州府巨野县身亡。据称，此二人长期以来热衷于帮助当地教众反抗不信教者之迫害，因而遭到"大刀会"报复，为 20 名匪徒残忍杀害。正如道格拉斯先生等人所言，"此一暴力行径绝非中国政府所为，概因当时之中国政府对外国传教士十分友好，断然不会加害外国友人。"③然德国政府完全无视实情，竟而怀疑该事件为原山东巡抚李秉衡煽动

---

① 在德国侵占胶州湾之际，《柏林最新报道》扬言，德国与法国及俄罗斯一道参与解决中日纠纷之目的绝非为了加强法国及俄罗斯在华势力，而是为了促进自身之利益。
② 科迪尔，《历史》，第 3 卷，第 343—347 页。
③ 道格拉斯，《欧洲与远东》，第 318 页。

策划。接到德国教会激进分子、德国政府死忠人士普特曼·韦勒的消息，安策尔主教第一时间将事件告知德国驻华公使冯·海靖，后者随即向德皇弗雷德里希大帝汇报。隔天冯·海靖就得到指令，要求抓住机会扩大事态，一如政府电令所言："索取极致之赔偿"，且"无轻言满意之条件"。① 另一方面，清政府迅速下令搜捕，并于三周后成功抓获四名凶徒。

然，德方接到捕获嫌犯之消息数小时后，即由棣德利率德军分乘恺撒号、威廉王妃号和鸬鹚号三艘巡洋舰于11月11日从吴淞口出发，并于14日抵达胶州湾。棣德利给时任胶州湾守将章高元去电，称一支强大德军将要登陆胶州湾并"借地操练"。章高元随即遵北京【原文使用Peking字样。Peking为威妥玛拼音，对应中文为"北京"二字。威妥玛拼音为先后担任过英国驻华公使馆汉文正使、驻华使馆参赞和驻华全权公使（1869—1882）的威妥玛（Thomas Francis Wade，1818—1895）所创。在1860年签订的《中英北京条约》（Convention of Peking）和1909年修建的京张（北京—张家口）铁路在英文中都使用Peking对应中文"北京"二字，而当时的北京仍是清政府的"（京师）应天府"，至1914年陶文撰写和提交时北洋政府仍然依清制将北京称作"应天府"。本译文依惯例将陶文中的Peking一般仍译作"北

---

① 哈丁，《见地》，1914年11月11日周三刊，第579页。赖因施先生在其《世界政治》第33页中有言，"法德之间为获取保护东方罗马天主教传教士资格而进行之斗争，明确体现罗马天主教之势力"。法国一直充当东方天主教徒保护者角色；而德国则始终试图通过对梵蒂冈施加影响来打破此一垄断。德皇甚至宣称，惟有德国才是德国传教士团体唯一保护国。如今我们已然清楚，所谓"保护国"在中国问题上是何种意味：德皇要求中国对在胶州湾意外身亡之德国传教士进行赔偿，并试图以此"暴力行径"为借口在中国获得永久驻留之地。德国也曾试图从梵蒂冈教廷获取在巴勒斯坦和叙利亚之宗教保护国权益而未果；然德国坚持宣称"保护世界各地之德国传教士乃德国一向奉行之原则，亦为德国权力之所在"。且德国并非唯一利用本国传教士获利之国家。其余野心勃勃之国家在一定程度上也践行着"国旗随使命而动，贸易随国旗而行"之原则。譬如，法国利用佩雷-贝瑟洛特事件强行索取在云南之特许权即为另一清晰例证。

第二章 胶州湾

京",只有在涉及"驻 Peking 公使"时,才译作"驻华公使"。——译者注】政府敕令撤离胶州湾。随后,600 名德国海军陆战队官兵入驻胶州湾军营。

德方所作所为自然有违国际公法。德军登陆胶州湾前未与中国政府交涉,然状若久已在两国间达成共识。和平时期派遣军兵登陆友国海岸,且试图征占其领土之一部分,断非 19 世纪文明之国家应有之行为。无疑,此一行径非常有损德意志帝国之国际形象。

德军登陆胶州湾当天,德国政府宣称[①],德国一贯秉持与中国友好之原则,且无任何侵占中国领土之图谋[②],然无意于归还已借驻之胶州湾,除非中国就两位德国传教士意外身亡事件做出相应赔偿。仅数日后,德国驻华公使冯·海靖向中国外交部提出一长串赔偿要求。

要求包括:(一)为此一事件中遭遇戕劫之德国传教士立碑纪念;(二)对遇害者家属予以赔偿;(三)因谋杀案发生在其辖境内,将山东巡抚李秉衡革职查办;(四)赔偿德国出兵胶州湾之费用;(五)涉案嫌犯及一应地方官绅均需从严从重惩处;(六)山东如有开办铁路及于铁路就近开采煤矿事宜,中国应先准允德国商人及工程师承办。德国租借胶州湾之图谋已隐然待发。[③]

中国外交部虽同意上述要求,但作为交换条件,要求德军撤离胶州湾,不料遭到德方拒绝。德方称,在得到中方进一步保证前,德军需保护中国范围内德国侨民安全。以此为由,德国正式公开表达其租借胶州湾及其他中国内陆领土之意愿,此一表态无疑与德国先前的声明背道而驰。

与此同时,德意志帝国普鲁士王子、德皇胞弟亨利受命统领远征军前往中国。1897 年 12 月 15 日远征军启航,德国皇帝在基尔城堡设

---

① 《日本每周邮报》,1897 年,第 561 页,第 646 页。
② 德国租借行为符合其声明否?
③ 《美国总统咨文及外交关系》,1898 年,第 188 页。

宴为亨利王子饯行。德皇向亨利王子举杯敬酒，曰："吾等神圣之祖父及其伟大之总理励精图治；吾等之父皇浴血沙场，封疆扩土。汝此次远征乃基于父辈伟业之必然结果；亦为吾辈新近统一而崛起之德意志帝国跨洋殖民目标达成之首战。当此我国商贸勃兴之时，惟有置于帝国力量保护之下，方能平稳繁荣发展……帝国实力取决于远洋力量，远洋力量与帝国实力相互依存，缺一不可。要使移居海外之德国侨民放心，汝等无论身处何地均受帝国之保护；无论何人胆敢侵犯汝等正当权利或施加人身伤害，都将遭遇铁血还击。而今天降大任于吾弟，弟虽弱冠，面对磨难，淡定从容，具无上荣光，可顺应德国万众心意，加冕称王。"亨利王子巧妙回应道："传播吾皇之福音于四海系吾此行唯一之目的。无论得遇倾听与否，吾当竭尽全力，铭刻此福音于吾达到之每一地方。"①

此番基尔城堡对话听起来更像文明戏中英雄人物之对白，如非亵渎上帝，亦属不可理喻，委实滑稽可笑。然对话无疑清晰表明德国对远东地区之态度。虽无实质性内容，此番对话却足以加速德国强占胶州湾之步伐。越两月，时值1898年1月5日，胶州湾租借条约正式签订；② 逾四月，光绪帝正式会见亨利王子。

德国治下之租借地政府

胶州湾自租借后其行政管理交与德国海军处置，由一名德国海军军官出任"首脑"，名曰总督。租借地政府之政务委员会由所有行政部门负责人组成，受总督及其他四人监督。此四人选自平民，任期两年：其中一名经委员会同意由总督直接任命；另一名来自在华外企

---

① 此二者对话之全文皆刊登于《日本每周邮报》，1898年，第85—88页。
② 1898年3月6日，清政府代表李鸿章、翁同龢及德使冯·海靖在北平签署《中德胶澳租借条约》，见赫茨莱特，《中国条约》，第1卷，第350页。

职员；再一人国籍不限，但需从纳税人中挑选，且此人至少应交付不低于 50 美元之地税；第四人选需来自商务委员会。此外，租借地政府部门还设有专为欧洲侨民服务之司法官员，必要时可向德国驻上海领事法院提交诉状；而当地中国居民只有在极特殊情况下才适用此管理法条。

德占胶州湾后之政策

厘清德国侵占胶州湾之过程，自然不难推断其管理政策之基调。从棣德利发表的中文声明中亦可见一斑："众所周知，吾奉德国君主命率部进抵胶州湾，本意即将此海湾及附属之海岛、领地纳入德皇治下。尔等不可有无谓之举，违抗当局命令。尔等既已身陷'囚笼'，当知抵抗徒劳，不仅于当下处境无丝毫助益，惟加速尔等灭亡而已。"[1]

一如其他列强，德国亦是野心勃勃，欲将其天才民族烙印铭刻至世界每一角落。此种意愿与生俱来，属德意志民族之本性，深植于心。此亦德人久欲于中国实施之野心。于德人而言，于异国他乡可以听闻本族语言，抑或令异族认可德意志民族之习俗与制度，内心自是志得意满。此外，此举可令他国仰视德国之威严与国力，意义尤为重大。冯·布洛埃亦曾发言，虽略去其余两点，但却对最后一点加以充分阐释："在我辈眼中，德国战舰与军队驻扎胶州湾才是对未来发展最强有力之保证。为此，德意志帝国需不断向地方当局及中国人展现威压"。[2]

---

[1]《泰晤士报》，1898 年 1 月 6 日。
[2] 同上，1898 年 1 月 25 日。种种事实表明，德国在胶州湾施行之管理未曾丝毫顾忌中国居民权利与感受。一切政策均为德国人着想。在欧战爆发前，胶州湾实质上可以看作德国领土。至于当地之中国人，虽纳税日重，却无权参与任何管理事务。此即为何胶州湾之德国人唤作"红魔鬼"也。但须注意，与俄国人及日本人在关东施行之管理相比，德国人在胶州湾之行政管理属实温和合理许多。

再次论及德国侵占胶州湾一事，冯·布洛埃大放厥词："吾等既已在胶州湾奠定自身之战略及政治地位，自可确保对远东未来发展产生决定性影响。处此有利地位，吾等自可信心满满看待国际事务发展。德国外交将在东方走出一条属于自身之从容、坚定、和平之道路。"

简而言之，德国在胶州湾建立永久性商业中心及海军基地之过程中，丝毫未曾顾及中方利益，对中国施以武力威胁，恣意提出条件，最终希望以胶州湾为据点建立自身势力及利益范围。为更好地理解德国实行之政策，有必要简要梳理中德之间制定之条约及公约，其一同界定了胶州湾事件涉及之范围。此外，还需对德国人此间所作所为做一概览，从中可见德国政策之实质。

条约及公约精要

首先，中国有权向德国政府收取租借胶州湾之租金。但是，德国人认为所谓租金只是一种形式。冯·布洛埃在国会讲话中提到此事。他说："德国无需支付大额租金，概因此次租借并非等值支付租赁之土地，而仅为法律意义上一种认缴行为，无非从理论上承认中国皇帝对该地区之所有权。"[1]

根据1906年中德公约，[2] 清政府帝国海关总署负责收取胶州湾关税，而该地区之海关关长需由德国驻华公使会同清政府帝国海关总署署长共同任命。

简而言之，德国租借胶州湾193平方英里领土[3]，在租借期内中国政府放弃行使主权，但可收取微薄租金并保有部分征收关税权利。除此之外，德国可以在该土地上随心所欲、恣意而为。

---

[1] 演讲全文参见《日本每周邮报》，1898年3月26日，第326页。
[2] 详情参阅《作为港口之胶州湾》一文。
[3] 赫茨莱特，《中国条约》，第352页。

第二章 胶州湾

而在胶州湾高水位区方圆 50 公里中立区内，中国人基本保留一切行政管理权，惟以下两点例外：其一，中国虽有权在该区域内驻扎军队或采取其他军事行动，但前提为中方必须与德国政府达成一致意见，且必须保证德军可在中立区内自由通行；其二，未经德国政府事先同意，中国不得采取任何措施或颁布任何法令。至于涉及采矿及铁路特许权之四项条款，更是欲将中国置于绝望无助之境地。中国商人的确可能在德国在华商会中占有一定股份，而该商会之成立意在负责修建两条割让之铁路线。① 此外，中德双方商人的确可能是以合资方式共同负责铁路沿线 10 英里范围内之煤炭开采。然《中德胶澳租借条约》最后一项明确指出："如果中国在山东省境内筹划之事务需外国资金、援助或人员，中国同意首先求助德国商人，咨询其有否意愿负责该工程并提供所需材料。换言之，只有在无需借助外国资本且德国政府和资本家不愿参与之情况下，才允许中国在自己之领土上自主处理相关事宜【条款原文为："在山东省内如有开办各项事务，商定向外国招集帮助为理，或用外国人，或用外国资本，或用外国料物，中国应许先问该德国商人等愿否承办工程，售卖料物。如德商不愿承办此项工程及售卖料物，中国可任凭自便另办，以昭公允"——译者注】。总之，铁路建设权与煤矿开采权之割让实质上已预示着德国已开始尝试在中国内陆地区建立自己之势力范围。

最后，如德国在租借期满前有意将胶州湾归还给中国，则中国将陷于进退维谷之艰难境地。该项条款规定："在将来某一租期未满之时，德国（而非中国）意欲归还胶州湾，则中国需支付德国在胶州湾花费之一切费用；且需选择另一合适地区割让给德国【条款原文为："嗣后如德国租期未满之前，自愿将胶澳归还中国，德国所有在胶澳费项，中国应许赔还，另将较此相宜之处，让与德国"——译者注】。"

---

① 详情参阅"与胶州湾相关之铁路"。

该条款尽显德国两大图谋：（一）彼时德国已在中国腹地建立自身势力范围，即便归还胶州湾，其不可避免仍将受到德国牵制，中国将无力控制该曾经割让之领土。但于德国而言，又可侵占另一心仪之地区，并利用所获赔偿新建商业及政治中心，从而启动另一在华势力范围。（二）必须牢记，德国租借胶州湾旨在保护德国在华利益不受损害，然德国此举确能保障胶州湾地区之安全乎？毫无疑问，德国已尽己所能在胶州湾建立坚固之堡垒。但若德国与其他列强，特别是与英国或日本突发意外冲突，德国能保障胶州湾地区之安全否？因此，一向谨慎之日耳曼民族可谓未雨绸缪，条款之规定系保障意外发生之时德国人可以从胶州湾全身而退。德国前一图谋也许无达成之可能，而后一图谋则充分体现出德国人之老谋深算。事实上，未等德国人表达其归还胶州湾之意愿，日本人已率先采取行动。

德国开发胶州湾资费总览

在德国租借之前，胶州湾仅有一500余人之小村庄。想要开发胶州湾，无疑困难重重，耗资极巨。然，德国在胶州湾之投入，类其于喀麦隆、多哥兰等地之举，充分展现其进取之态度，不懈之努力，以及敢冒风险之狮虎之心。

自1899年始至1914年止（时年胶州湾落入日本之手），德国年均拨款约1,000万马克开发胶州湾，而胶州湾年均支出为1,300万马克。在德国人管辖之下，胶州湾财政开销最大年度为1905—1906年，时年总支出为15,296,000马克，其中德国政府拨款达1,400万马克。前后15年间，德意志帝国政府总共拨款15,600万马克，而15年间胶州湾总支出为18,500万马克。下表详细列有开发胶州湾所费之巨额资金：

第二章 胶州湾

时间	支出 （马克）	德意志帝国拨款 （马克）
1899—1900	8,500,000	8,500,000
1900—1901	9,780,000	9,780,000
1901—1902	12,528,000	
1902—1903	12,876,000	12,168,000
1903—1904	13,088,000	12,421,000
1904—1905	15,296,000	12,583,000
1905—1906	13,278,000	14,000,000
1906—1907		11,735,000
1907—1908		
1908—1909	12,327,000	10,601,600
1909—1910	12,352,597	
1910—1911	12,722,000	
1911—1912	13,540,000	7,704,000
1912—1913	16,640,000	8,293,000
1913—1914	16,783,625	9,560,000

根据上表可知，除1902—1907年间，德国提高拨款数额以资助港口和其他重大工程建设，其余年份德国政府拨款一直稳定在700万马克至1,100万马克之间，且收支成比例增加。开支巨大证明该地区发展繁荣，而财政收入同步增长则表明胶州湾正逐步发展成为自给自足之地。胶州湾很有可能如香港一般，每年财政收支相抵且有盈余。然而后来之事实证明，此间种种努力最终却为一直虎视眈眈之日本做了嫁衣。

如需了解财政支出明细以及财政收入来源，可从1905—1906年度预算中获悉一二。该年度胶州湾商贸蓬勃发展，具体数据如下：

胶州湾年度预算（1905年4月1日—1906年3月31日）

一、收入（单位：英镑）

土地销售额	2,447
直接税收	4,406
其他收入	24,279
帝国资助	717,607
收入总计	748,739

二、支出（单位：英镑）

经常性支出

民政管理	53,928
海军管理	74,257
驻华派遣军	1,346
军粮	30,894
服装	10,655
大炮和防御工事	15,595
公共建筑维修	17,685
马鞍和马车	8,865
公众礼拜和教育	3,493
医院和医疗卫生服务	17,698
财政	5,586
各种事务	53,556
退休基金	441
经常性支出小计	293,999

第二章 胶州湾

临时支出

港湾工程	170,004
建材及土地购置	96,138
工业住宅	4,895
林业和河流管理	3,916
军备	122,375
航标和斟测	1,958
第五次浮动船坞装置	53,845
意外费用	1,609
临时支出小计	453,640
支出总计	748,739

从上面内容可知，总支出 748,739 英镑中，有 223,849 英镑用于建造海港和浮动船坞，222,438 英镑用于军事和海军工程，仅有 53,928 英镑用于民政管理。港口及码头与海军管理直接相关，因此，总开支有约 60% 用于军事和海军事务；所涉防御工事、港口及码头需连续多年建设方能完工。

此外，山东铁路公司于 1899 年 6 月成立，资本为 5,400 万马克（约合 270 万英镑），用于修建铁路。两家著名的矿业公司——山东矿业公司和德国国外矿业协会——相继成立，专营煤矿开采；前者由一些权势滔天之德国银行家组建，资本为 1,200 万马克（约合 60 万英镑），而后者则由"殖民地商业联合会"——一家由德国联邦参议院授权之特许公司——成立之协会。

因此，自 1898 年"租借"该地直到日后为日本所侵占，德国政府及其所监管之铁路及矿业公司开发胶州湾共花费 123,575,000 美元，该笔款项约相当于 1904 年前俄罗斯在"满洲"投资（257,500,000 美元）之五成。

德意志亚洲银行（资本达 500 万两白银）会同一些小型企业，如山东商会（资本 24 万马克）和胶州湾商会（资本 20.4 万马克）等，也积极投身胶州湾之开发。

结果证明，于德国人而言租借胶州湾实属奢侈，但他们又似乎觉得物有所值，毕竟收入大幅度增长符合他们对"奢侈品消费"之期待。正如凯勒先生所言："借此奢侈之举，德人顿觉于世界眼中，德意志帝国得以彰显显贵。"

除了将大量资本投入胶州湾开发外，德国还向胶州湾派出了一支由军官、士卒、工程师和淘金者组成之派遣军。来者自称德籍爱国人士，他们要在胶州湾播下种子，他们希望种子能茁壮成长，直至长成郁郁葱葱之德意志帝国大树，且具有"举世瞩目之东方特性"。

以上为德国租借胶州湾所费"心力"之情况总览。以下则是对其在胶州湾重大举动之详细介绍。

青岛口岸

胶州湾是整个租借地之总称，青岛则为其主要港口名称。1895 年 9 月 2 日，青岛宣告成为自由港，清政府帝国海关在青岛火车站设关收取关税。1906 年，一项新的公约生效，青岛失去自由港地位，如同在其他条约口岸一般，清政府帝国海关总署在青岛可收取关税；但该条约除其他不公平条款外，居然规定青岛海关收入之 20% 应交付德国政府。据 1912 年统计，青岛海关年入白银 1,670,029 两，其中竟有 334,006 两转交给德国人。中国租借胶州湾与德国人，所获租金微不足道，德国总理冯·布洛埃一言以蔽之，曰"确认付款"【确认胶州湾为租借地而支付的款项——译者注】。如今，土地所有者在自身领地上设立海关收取关税竟然一年要向土地租借者支付 334,006 两白银，岂非滑天下之大稽？然，在洛克希尔先生口中，此一变革为特殊情形下有利双方之特惠政策；经此改良，青岛海关替代胶州湾海关，为所涉商人及海关官员带来了便利，也增加了收入。[①] 凡此种种，再加上1909年青岛海关之新安排，的确为促进胶州湾商贸发展做出了些许贡献。下表可见1900年至1912年胶州湾之贸易增长：[②]

日期	进口（关制白银两）	出口（关制白银两）
1900	158,598	32,282
1901	2,527,609	18,370
1902	3,678,690	105,272
1903	5,134,229	234,216
1904	3,437,897	845,302
1905	4,372,937	2,430,350
1906	7,019,263	3,540,123
1907	7,297,944	887,226
1908	8,266,562	2,707,707
1909	10,655,398	3,359,386
1910	25,409,209	17,171,415
1911	26,287,988	19,853,669
1912	29,742,731	24,999,360

从1900年到1912年，胶州湾商贸总额增长280倍，而其海关收入则增长了300倍。在最后五年中，其海关收入从中国口岸城市第22位上升至第六位，此一独特记录表明其进出口贸易能力仅排在上海、天津、汉口、广州和汕头等口岸之后，位列第六。时年大连港海关收入达26万两白银，排在胶州湾之后，位列第七。当然，大连港发展速度甚至要快过胶州湾。大连港商贸总额1907年仅为140,738两，但1912年增至1,407,926两；胶州湾商贸总额1907年为934,623两，

---

① 《美国领事和贸易报告》，1906年，第179页。
② 《政治家年刊》，1902—1914年。

1912年为1,670,029两。在此期间，胶州湾同比收入增幅仅为大连港六分之一。此五年间，尽管大连港贸易额增长可与胶州湾相提并论，但仍可肯定地说，中国除大连港外，再无口岸城市贸易额增长可以超过胶州湾；且可以断言，除大连及上海外，中国再无口岸城市发展速度可与胶州湾比肩。

然而，必须注意到该口岸城市之商贸始终无法彻底摆脱其创建时人为添加之条件，其贸易繁荣始终或多或少依赖于德国政府之投入。时有报道称，日本入主胶州湾后始终无力恢复其商贸繁荣，如此种报道属实，则可证明胶州湾先天底蕴之不足。

作为海军基地之胶州湾

胶州湾向来享有山东天然海洋门户美名，实可谓中国山东之海上枢纽；此乃德国多年来在中国海域觊觎之目标。既然"帝国霸权源自远洋实力"，如欲实现德皇之野心，夺取此一天然良港自是至关重要，嗣后在胶州湾兴建海军基地也早已纳入德人考虑之中。

果然，德人甫一接管胶州湾管理权，即从国内派遣一支由工程师及熟练工匠组成的队伍开赴胶州湾兴建早已设计完成之庞大防御工事。德国工程队建造了一个由12个现代堡垒组成之环形工事，从北部高耸之多岩石崂山半岛，沿距离青岛港6英里之岛后方茂密山脊延伸，再沿灵山南部半岛铺开。德人又耗费700万美元疏通海港和海湾；所建造之浮动船坞可起吊1.6万吨货物。德人又建造了一座2,000米长的下沉式花岗岩码头；并建造一现代化船坞，可停靠当今世界之最大商船和甲舰。十年间，德人于港口工程一事耗资逾3,000万美元。德人所设海军基地既可用于海军事务，亦可用于商业贸易，基地之内尚可造船：事实上，只需备足原材料，基地内有可能建造和装备多艘二等巡洋舰。1908年建造之军营可容纳5,000名士卒。最初德国向胶州湾海军基地派驻3,000人，至一战前，派遣军人数不断增加。负责日常防务之常规部队人数超过6,000，另从在华德国侨民挑选出2,500名志愿者，整支部队由1个骑兵中队、1个野战炮兵连、2个机枪连、5个海军炮兵连、一个包含4个飞行编组之航空队和一个本土预备役连构成。① 赴胶州湾服役在德国广受欢迎，家世背景优良之年轻人纷纷报名入伍，其目的不仅是为国出力，亦可同时满足自身对于远东之好奇心矣。

直至本世纪第二个十年，租借地之军事目的才开始为工业需求让路，而原本工业目的一直属于德人租借并开发胶州湾之长远目标。确切地说，直至前年（1913年），柏林帝国国库年均划拨给胶州湾1,300万马克预算款，其中约有1,000万马克用于军事之特别开支。据说，管理胶州湾之普鲁士官员每花费1美元于平民事务中则必投入10美元于军事工程之上。

如今，靠近青岛港之潍县及博山煤矿年均产量虽仅有50万吨，但足以令胶州湾成为甲舰与其他船只理想之燃料补给站。

此外，一家德国开发公司——山东铁路公司——决定斥资1,200万美元在青岛建立一座大型钢铁厂。此一决定令德国人觉得自己制定之宏伟目标已日渐付诸实施，且已初见成效。在1914年6月5日召开之同次会议上，该开发公司决定除钢铁厂外再新建一座兵工厂。一旦建设完工，该项工程可进一步推动胶州湾成为远东最强大之海军基地及军事要塞。

连接胶州湾之铁路

德国经济学家弗雷德里克·李斯特早就提出了政治与商业发展互通之原则；此一原则在胶州湾展现得淋漓尽致。德国野心勃勃，意欲

---

① 《见地》，1914年11月11日刊，第582页。

将胶州湾打造成第二个旧金山,并在山东省境内建立自身之势力范围,借此控制广袤之中国内陆。德国意图如何实现此一谋划?缺乏大面积覆盖之铁路网自难实现此一目标,须知帝国霸权不仅源自远洋实力,亦来自铁路线之控制权。于是乎胶州湾便呈现殊为诡谲之一幕:德意志帝国之霸权正沿着海陆两大交通线在中国蔓延。

除租借胶州湾外,德国亦胁迫中国允其在山东境内修建两条铁路线:一条铁路线自胶州湾始,经潍县、青州、博山、淄川、松坪再到济南和山东边境;另一条铁路线从胶州湾到沂州,再经莱芜到泰安。济南至山东边境铁路需等主干线完工且路线勘定后方能修建。① 后沂州至济南铁路线计划遭搁置,取而代之者为英德集团资助并由中国政府管理之中国皇家津浦铁路。② "今对胶州湾至沂州铁路线加以勘测,决议放弃原拟修建之计划。"③ 至此,德国仅需考虑自胶州湾始,经潍县、博山至济南之铁路线。

该铁路线由总部位于德国柏林之山东铁路公司经营,总资本为5,400 万马克。1904 年 6 月,此一从青岛通往济南、长 256 英里之主线路开始通车。1910 年,昌县—博山及赵川—泰川两条支线铁路相继通车。至此,连接胶州湾之铁路线总长达 310 英里。④

自主干线开通之日起,该铁路沿线商业逐渐繁荣。"这不足为奇。胶州湾自拥有一流之港口及铁路,交通线便连接起该地区和世界上人口最稠密国家之心脏地带,此乃前无古人之创举。因此,胶州湾之繁荣自有其道理。"⑤ 胶州湾年贸易额已在前一节讨论过,以下考察铁路主干线启用所带来之贸易份额:

---

① 赫茨莱特,《中国条约》,第一卷,第 353 页。
② 《远东评论》,1909 年 11 月刊,第 286 页。
③ 同上。
④ 《中国年鉴》,1914 年,第 213 页。
⑤ 《美亚协会杂志》,1915 年 1 月刊,第 367 页。

第二章 胶州湾

日期	年客运量（人）	年货运量（吨）	年净利润（马克）
1904	558,868	179,270	
1905	803,527	310,482	2,063,572
1906	846,000	381,000	2,642,000
1911	909,065	717,189	4,731,238
1912	1,230,043	852,001	7,050,000

从以上数据可知，1904—1912 的 8 年间，胶州湾铁路客运量增长一倍有余，货运量增长逾 4 倍，而净利润增长了 3.5 倍。客货流量逐步增长预示着胶州湾未来之商贸额必将更为可观。如 1912 年德国国库划拨胶州湾开发款项为 700 万马克，而该年度胶州湾商贸净利润高达 770.4 万马克【原文如此，与表格中数字不符——译者注】，净利润已足以补偿德国国库划拨之补助款。

该铁路干线通车也直接影响了中国通商口岸烟台之贸易，具体状况如下表所示：①

日期	进口贸易额（关制白银两）	出口贸易额（关制白银两）
1905	9,607,561	4,677,509
1906	7,906,839	4,806,654
1907	6,620,215	3,299,002
1908	6,182,640	3,524,592
1909	5,999,755	4,037,687
1910	15,464,159	14,731,624
1911	16,654,026	13,916,518
1912	15,872,719	12,863,731

---

① 《政治家年刊》，1907—1914 年。

从上表中可知，自胶州湾铁路通车以来，烟台进口贸易额从白银 9,607,561 两下降至 5,999,755 两，出口量则从 4,677,509 两降至 4,037,687 两。自 1910 年以来①，由于津浦铁路北段通车，烟台贸易额突然增加，但自此之后，其贸易额几乎保持不变，而与此同时，胶州湾贸易额却增加了 20%。②

从下表可以看出胶州湾之勃兴及烟台港之没落：③

日期	芝罘海关收入（关制白银两）	胶州湾海关收入（关制白银两）
1905	871,607	545,150
1906	818,322	863,430
1907	633,243	934,623
1908	644,914	926,716
1909	748,338	1,120,243
1910	651,265	1,238,394
1911	595,914	1,251,001
1912	704,735	1,670,029

根据中国各海关贸易总额排名，1905—1912 年间，在全部 47 个港口中，胶州湾港口贸易量排名从第 16 位上升至第 6 位，而烟台港则从第 10 位下降至第 14 位。

不惟烟台海关收入呈下降趋势，而与烟台海关相互依存之地方税收下降幅度更为明显。1909 年，其地方税收仅收入 97,609 两，到了 1910 年实际收入仅 76,262 两。1911 年烟台地方税收略有上升，而到了 1912 年竟暴跌至 68,823 两。

---

① 《中国年鉴》，1914 年，第 223 页。
② 同上。
③ 同上，第 139 页及 122 页。然而，必须承认，根据最近之海关报告，烟台海关 1912—1913 年贸易额出现小幅增长，且商业形势平稳。

同样情况亦出现在稻草编织品贸易行业。1903年，在山东两港出口之此类国产货品中，烟台港出口量占总量70%，胶州湾港口仅占30%。从此一显著变化中可以看出，在出口领域，胶州湾港口已然完全取代烟台港。从下表中可以更为清楚地看出此一现象：①

日期	胶州湾（单位：美担）	烟台（单位：美担）
1908	99,701	930
1909	125,315	388
1910	119,068	225
1911	104,764	5

【原文单位为cwt，即"美担"，是美制质量单位，20美担＝2000磅＝907.186千克＝1美吨——译者注】

凭借铁路优势，青岛港抢走了烟台港几乎所有生丝及花生贸易。

德国在山东攫取之铁路特许权另一直接之重大影响体现在津浦铁路建设方案中。1897年，容闳博士获得津镇铁路特许建设权，并获准谋求外国资金援助。容闳博士原本与英美资本家谈判，达成一项估价2,700万美元之黄金贷款计划。②1898年，容闳博士之宏大融资计划获批数月之后，德国强行介入，意欲凭刚刚获得之铁路特许权废除容闳博士之引资计划。德人所提要求显然有违条约，因为条约规定德国只有在条约签订后之涉外贷款项目中才拥有优先权。但最终，德国断绝了容闳博士及美国资本家之希望。1898年，正式协议签字盖章，规定铁路之建设及管理权交由中国政府，由英德两国财团提供500万英镑贷款、部分物资以及工程技术人员。然而，英德两国首席工程师均应受中国项目总经理管控。

---

① 《下议院会议报告》，1912—1913年，第95卷，第79页，第183页。
② 《远东评论》，1909年11月刊，第309页。

厘清青岛—济南铁路特许权之影响后，以下可分析铁路连接给青岛带来之显赫地位。

首先，通过津浦铁路北段（390.5英里）、北平至沈阳铁路（527英里）、京张铁路（124英里）、中国东部铁路（1081英里）以及跨西伯利亚铁路等线路，津济铁路将青岛与天津、北平、沈阳、张家口、圣彼得堡、柏林和欧洲其他地方连接起来。通过绥远县、大同府和库伦之京张铁路扩建工程（600英里）将青岛和跨西伯利亚铁路海拉尔地段紧密连接起来。津浦铁路南段（236.5英里）连接青岛和中国古都南京；沪宁铁路（193英里）和江浙铁路（241英里）将青岛与上海、杭州和宁波连接起来。经南昌跨越长江至潮州之规划线路及潮汕线，可于汕头抵达福建海岸。1913年底，德国政府宣布与中国签订协议修建其他铁路线路。首先，高密—汉川线会将更多的铁、煤、大豆和小麦运往青岛。其次，德国计划在济南和顺德之间修建一条铁路线（755英里），连接津浦铁路和京汉铁路。① 这将使青岛与汉口（所谓中国之芝加哥）直接连接，并通过规划中之汉粤铁路，与广州间接连接起来。兖州至开封铁路线计划尤为重要：兖州已通过津浦铁路与青岛连接，德国密谋连接兖州与开封，以便未来青岛可以通过规划中之西北大干线直接与河南、潼关、西安、兰州及伊犁等地相连。如此，便如哈丁先生所言："终有一天，它会从突厥斯坦广袤而又鲜为人知之沙漠中穿过三千英里外俄罗斯里海前哨，刺穿亚洲大陆心脏，复从那里穿过中国之内陆地区，直达太平洋；另一方面，它将通过计划中之西安—重庆—云南—法国中印线与重庆、成都和法国中印线相连接。此番计划已得到中国政府同意并签署相关协议。早在1910年，德国人就已对作为津浦铁路德国段支线之兖州—开封线路加以勘察。目前该线路终点为青州，但规划之线路最终将抵达开封。一旦青岛拥有庞大之铁

---

① 《中国年鉴》1914年，第210页

路交通网络,再加上其天然良港,自然会成为此一庞大交通系统之最终口岸。"

根据以上分析,可以得出结论,一旦此庞大铁路系统建成,青岛向北、向南、向西之铁路运输能力将十分强劲。一如【日本人】在东北一样,德国人在青岛对每一件事都拟订了详细之计划,种种事实都表明德国人对青岛野心勃勃。①

德国在胶州湾之其他作为

前文已经指出,德国租借胶州湾之野心远非建设一个商业中心和海军基地而已,更是要在中国腹地建立其势力范围。前文已对德国之军务及铁路事业加以分析,以下将对德国租借胶州湾之其他作为加以探讨。

(一)煤矿开采。德人所获之铁路特许权通常附有铁路沿线之采矿权。《中德条约》规定德国可以在铁路沿线30公里范围内开采煤矿。但是,正如威尔先生所言,德人踏足之领域远超条约限制。至1912年,德国在华煤矿年产量逐年上升,时年增至50多万吨,占当年世界产煤总量之$\frac{1}{2330}$。各年度具体年产量如下表所示:

日期	范图兹矿(单位:吨)	恒山矿(单位:吨)	总量(单位:吨)
1907	145,000	34,200	179,200
1908	222,450	56,600	279,050
1909	272,000	160,000	432,000
1910	230,064	252,816	482,880
1911	184,233	302,300	486,533
1912			573,676

---

① 该部分数据基于《中国年鉴》修订之数据,1914年,第208—244页。

（二）拓荒与耕种。 德国在胶州湾与其在其他租借地一样，最有价值之科学考察与当地行政当局之拓荒耕种同步进行，突出体现在植树造林工作中。德人在胶州湾开垦有 144 英亩土地，每年向当地人出售 100 万棵树木和植物。德人在胶州湾之拓荒与耕种卓有成效，每年可从其中获得约 10 万马克的收入。①

　　（三）邮局。 德国邮政业务成功入侵中国内陆。德国铁路公司每列火车上，都留有一节车厢交由德国邮政公司使用。德国邮政通过降低邮费来保持对中国邮政之竞争优势。

　　（四）咨政。 威尔先生就曾指出，德国人一直努力尝试让山东巡抚正式任命一名德国外交顾问。

　　（五）传教。 "同在西非一样"，切拉达姆先生说，"德国传教士向来是德国势力渗透之先遣队。"② 他甚至把传教士团体列入政府外派机构。事实上，山东天主教主教安泽宣称，能否占领胶州湾于德国传教士而言乃生死攸关之问题。③ 为了刺激德国民众对加入传教使团及前往殖民地之热情，德国教授米尔布特公开宣称："传教及殖民政治乃我辈之使命，吾等理当相信签订殖民地条约将有利德意志帝国之发展。"④

　　现今驻胶州湾之德国传教士使团包含 15 支普通使团和 3 支特遣使团。尽管笔者相信他们中部分人目的纯正、一心向教；但仍有部分人因为从政府接受财政援助而被迫一边为上帝服务，一边替帝国工作。⑤

　　（六）教育。 如不能树立德国文化之主导地位，租借地则无法完

---

① 《下议院会议报告》，1912—1913 年，第 75—183 卷。
② 切拉达姆，《殖民地与德国殖民地》，第 127 页。
③ 参照冯·布洛埃演讲，《日本每周邮报》，1898 年 3 月刊。
④ 米尔布特，《殖民政治之使命》，第 4 页和第 71 页。
⑤ 《德国殖民系统》，第 3 页。

成其德国化之进程。于是德人尝试通过建立德式学校完成此一进程。一位作家曾评论道:"青岛之学校与体育馆比任何同等规模城镇都多。"①"中国人和欧洲人严格分离。有九所学校由德国政府全资创立。殖民地之意志由学校支配。"米尔布特先生说:"世界各国人民都需要接受更好之教育,尤其需要学好德语。"②当然,不容否认,一些中国青年学子也在这些德式学校获得科学启蒙,激发了科研灵感。

(七)土地问题。如不能完全剥夺中国人之土地所有权,就不可能令胶州湾完全落入德国手中。胶州湾之中国人若想出售土地,惟有卖与德国政府,再俟德国政府转售殖民地上之欧洲人——此间欧洲人士大部亦为德国人。③土地购买者须缴纳33%之购置税。如拥有之土地25年内仍没有出售,则土地所有者必须发布通知,拟订土地销售计划。而政府可以优先购买即将出售之土地。每位地产拥有者每年须缴付地产资本价值6%之税款。如果某地产未在土地使用年限之前建造,则业主自然丧失产权,而德国政府只需要支付土地评估价值五成资金即可占有该地产。1903年12月31日发布之法令改变了这种情况,该法令规定了土地拥有者支付累进之土地增值税,而不是丧失产权。总而言之,德国政府一直试图以25年为期,强行从中国人手中夺走对胶州湾土地之全部控制权。④显然,如同德国在波兰之行径,在胶州湾,德人以税收为手段,逐步占有所有土地控制权。有德国人甚至为此辩护称:"如此一来,租借地内土地投机活动被禁,而租借地政府也掌握了土地政策的控制权。"⑤

---

① 《美亚协会杂志》,1915年1月刊,第365页。
② 米尔布特,《殖民政治下的使命》,第158页。
③ 科洪,《掌控太平洋》,第409页。
④ 《西方》,第70卷,第17—21页。
⑤ 格罗特沃德,《殖民地气候》,第181页。

德国治下胶州湾之主要特点

从上述胶州湾之各项描述中，可见德人在山东势力之强大，亦可见其固有缺陷。一方面，德国实际上已将胶州湾侵占，使之德国化。租借地政府一位工程师出身之委员曾绘声绘色地说："到处都是德国人。官员是德国人，语言是德国语，货币亦为德国币。此间货品①如非山东生产，则必从德国运来，从针头到电动起重机，无一例外。值得注意的是，此间并无洋泾浜德语。"②

然而，虽则德国在胶州湾极力推广德国民生之道，该租借地始终不过是一些德国官员和军卒旅居之所。据统计，1913年居于胶州湾之白人中有3,806名德国人，其中公务人员2,638名，占德国人口三分之二。该地区之文明繁荣多是刻意而为，繁文缛节颇多，行动受限。胶州湾各种规定与政策自是为了确保德意志帝国之直接利益。即便是德国商人亦发现德国官员对待本国商人，就像普鲁士军官对待手中新兵一般粗暴；此等军人大多不懂商务，且对商业利益不屑一顾。因此，胶州湾租借地在德国治下，其贸易发展与日本在大连和英国在香港之贸易相比望尘莫及。单看1910年德国在华贸易额及其在外国总贸易额占比即可得以证实：③

	德国贸易额（英镑）	总贸易额（英镑）	德国贸易占比（%）
进口	109,000	3,501,000	3.1
出口	17,000	2,369,000	0.7

基于上述种种原因，科洪先生得出如下结论：德国商人，无论其对殖民政策何其狂热，到目前为止，他们明显不愿在胶州湾定居或投

---

① 此间种种并非全为事实，应为德国人自我感觉良好所致。参见39页【原文】内容。
② 《美亚协会杂志》，1915年1月，第365页。
③ 哈德、加索尔，《德国远洋实力》，第288页。

资。① 哈特先生更是一语中的：胶州湾之德国居民几乎都是军兵和官吏；真正的德国殖民统治者不会出于信仰来到青岛。② 德国海外殖民有科学发展之传统，然殊为遗憾，德国之海外殖民却往往出于其他目的，以至于掩盖抵消其作为，令其科学之社会发展蒙羞。德意志帝国之专制思想当然是德国海外扩张之先天缺陷。如果德国商人亦可在中国通商口岸享受到如德国军人及官吏同样程度之最充分自由及礼遇，胶州湾自会更加繁荣。德国作家几乎一致谴责此等官僚主义，然正如德皇所言："吾辈欲在全球实现之丰功伟业，断无依仗笔墨实现之可能。"

---

① 科洪，《掌控太平洋》，第408页。
② 哈特，《关注东方》，第226页。

第三章

关东

第三章 关东

旅顺港、大连湾①和辽东半岛南部为俄罗斯租借地,并称关东地区,位于盛京省(今辽宁)最南端。该租借地面积约 1,256 平方英里,不包括中立区②和租借地周围水域。1898 年 3 月 26 日,沙俄从中国租借该地,成为关东地区管理者。1905 年元旦,俄国将军斯托塞尔对日投降,日本人接管关东地区;1905 年 12 月 22 日,中国与日本签订条约,正式承认该租借地之转让。

关东租借地与胶州湾不同之处在于:关东有两个港口,其一专事海军军务,另一港口可用于商业贸易;前者为旅顺港,后者为大连湾。

作为海军基地,旅顺港之重要性在中国海域可谓无出其右者。日俄战争中,日军经过 156 天的战斗方才从沙俄手中夺取旅顺港,其防御之坚固由此可见一斑。就防御能力而言,旅顺港仅次于塞瓦斯托波尔和普日茨密尔,塞瓦斯托波尔坚守 327 天始告陷落,而普日茨密尔坚守将近 200 天。③旅顺港是通往东北之门户,正如 203 高地是通往胶州湾之门户一般。由于更靠近首都,旅顺港之地位更为重要。

至于大连湾,自被日本占领以来,其商业贸易额之增长率超过中国所有其他港口,甚至包括胶州湾。故而朗霍姆先生所言非虚,理由充分,大连湾实可谓"东方之南安普顿"。

依托香港,九龙租借地之商业贸易额稳居中国各租借地之首;除此之外,关东各方面均为租借地翘楚。根据 1913 年统计数据,关东地区煤矿产量丰富,为胶州湾腹地煤矿产量 4 倍以上。关东地区境内铁路网全长 701 英里,长度为胶州湾德国铁路线总长 2.5 倍有余;整个关东铁路网由"南满洲铁道株式会"社直接控制,均与大连湾和旅顺港直接连接;与北京、汉城、张家口、营口、哈尔滨、符拉迪沃斯

---

① 大连湾又称作达尔尼或大连。
② 中立区位于租借地边界以北。其北部边界始于辽东西海岸的开州河河口,在余盐场以北经过塔阳河,并沿着该河左岸到达其河口,该河口以内属于中立区。
③ 《见地》,1915 年 3 月 31 日。

托克（海参崴）以及跨西伯利亚铁路线之连通远比胶济铁路线更为便捷。在关东，日本人对局势可谓一切尽在掌握，手段狠辣，令人咋舌。

旅顺口、大连湾与《中俄密约》

1896年秋，《中俄密约》①（简称《密约》）泄露，举世皆惊。该《密约》系沙俄驻华公使喀西尼提交中国政府之草案而已，然条款内容处处显露沙皇俄国染指我旅顺口及大连湾之企图。《密约》第十条竟然约定："位于辽东之旅顺、大连湾及其附属港湾乃重要之战略要地，中国有责任抓紧加强港口防御工事，修缮所有设施等，以防患于未然；如立此约，沙俄应提供一切必要援助以保护该地区不受任何外国势力侵占。中方应约束自己决不将其割让与他国；然，将来如遇要紧事，沙俄突然卷入战争，中国应允沙俄将陆海军暂时集结于上述港口以利沙俄坚守阵地、有效御敌【原文为："辽东之旅顺口以及大连湾等处地方，原系险要之处，中国极应速为整顿各事，以及修理各炮台等诸要务，以备不虞。既立此约，则俄国允准将此二处相为保护，不准他国侵犯。中国之允准，将来永不能让与他国占据。惟日后如俄国忽有军务，中国准将旅顺口及大连湾等处地方，暂行让与俄国水陆军营泊屯于此，以期俄军攻守之便"——译者注】。"《密约》自公布以来，究竟其为协商性草案抑或已经议定之永久条约，众说纷纭。然，中俄双方俱声称《密约》为无稽之谈，但《密约》内容与俄方现实图谋一致为不争之实，虽，双方政府均否认有商议该《密约》之行为。

旅顺口、大连湾与德国占领胶州湾

本文上一章中指出，《中俄密约》加速了德国占领胶州湾；反之，

---

① 《密约》全文参见威尔的《重塑远东》，第2卷，第439页。

第三章 关东

德国租借胶州湾亦加速沙俄对旅顺口及大连湾地区之操控。当德方突派先遣部队登陆胶州湾并升起德国国旗之时,俄国人愤怒之余亦感惊慌,为免两国起争端,无奈妥协。此时,德皇和沙皇之间举行了一次令人难忘之会晤。俄方何以为允协,自德国之视角简来云即:"我方取得胶州湾,盖愿得偿,且须一给煤港。我方既知,《中俄密约》为一协商性草案,而非已经议定之永久条约。自条约公布以来,已一年矣,而你方未曾采取措施以行其要。是故,我方不得不得出结论,你方已重新考虑了立场。宜如此,以我方不能亦不欲自胶州湾退;我方于远东有重利,须加固……沙俄之真正目标乃一不冻港,便即以铁路与沙俄领土相连接。你方势力源自人多势众,其力量必多于陆地施展,而非于海。以辽东半岛者尽为例:宜采用最直接之路线,将旅顺口及大连湾与横贯东北之贝加尔—海参崴之铁路线相连接,以此方可取据胶州湾而永不可得之有利地位。"① 因此,普特曼·韦勒有言,"俄国租赁【租借旅大港】协议以强且明者言径直取代《中俄密约》中昧违之言,此必直归因于德国与德国模式【租借胶州湾模式】之功。"

沙俄进占旅大港

在双方达成相互谅解协议之后,1897年12月18日,即德国占领胶州湾一月之后,3艘沙俄战舰进抵旅顺港。旋即,英国海军上将布勒率7艘舰艇抵达仁川济物浦,并派其中2艘舰艇前往旅顺港。然而,此一行动因遭遇俄方抗议被迫中止。4日后,莫拉维耶夫伯爵给出俄方解释,称其行动完全是为方便船只往来,与德国人占领胶州湾毫无关联。莫拉维耶夫伯爵进一步指出,虽然旅顺港条件得天独厚,有利于船只维修且冬季不结冰,但目前配备有强大破冰装置之海参崴仍将

---

① 威尔,《重塑远东》,第1卷,第344页。

继续成为俄国在远东之中心口岸。适时，除中国外，以英国人对沙俄之行动怀疑为剧。英国揪住沙俄外交部部长之声明，坚决要求开放大连湾，实施自由贸易。① 在一片反对声中，此一要求意在阻止沙俄占领旅顺口及大连湾，可谓直击命门，着实令沙俄恼羞成怒。俄国驻伦敦大使照会英国政府，视英国政府坚持开放大连湾之要求为侵犯沙俄在华势力范围，乃有意剥夺沙俄未来使用旅顺港之正当权利。与此同时，沙俄代办处告知北平总理衙门，假使允准开放大连湾为自由贸易口岸，必置沙俄于敌对势力。于是，英国与中国签订之租借协议并未涵盖大连湾。然沙俄仍不满意，始终尝试废除中英有关协议。1898年3月6日，中德双方签订《胶澳租借条约》；3月7日，俄方以与德方享有平等权利为借口，大胆提出长期以来之图谋：租借旅顺口和大连湾，并获得从绥芬河横贯满洲里至旅大港之铁路特许经营权。英国再次发出外交照会，指出旅顺港并非商业中心；倘若沙俄租借与西伯利亚大铁路相连之不冻港，英国并无异议；但若沙俄获得北京附近一军事港口控制权，英国必然全力反对。然而，沙俄毫不在意此类空洞威胁，于3月27日签署租借条约。②

沙俄治下之管理机构

据1899年之规定，关东行政属沙俄陆军部管辖，其行政中心设在旅顺港。行政首脑为关东总督，由兼任黑龙江、旅顺港和海参崴陆海军总司令之沙皇直接任命罢免。

大连湾以对外贸易开放为主，其组织和管理独立于关东地区。1899年7月30日，沙皇颁布一项命令，要求在大连湾附近建立一座"大

---

① 出自中英租借协议的一个条例。
② 赫茨莱特，《中国条约》，第1卷，第505页。

第三章　关东

连"新城。根据同年8月20日之暂行条例，该项工程由中东铁路公司承建，受财政部直接督导，并交由中央政府任命之行政长官主理，然需听命于关东总督。然而，1903年8月，沙俄又新拟行政安排，将关东与黑龙江省合并为一特区，此一状况维系至日俄战争。

关东条约之规定

沙俄租借关东之条约规定与德国租借胶州湾之条约规定虽略有不同，然大体一致。有关租借地内之防务、海军事务、民政事务以及中立区内中俄关系等条约规定，实质上与中德签订之有关条约规定一致。然而，局部差异的确存在。第一，若租借地内发生任何刑事案件，中国嫌犯移交至最近之中国官员处置；而在胶州湾，德国行政管理人员会受理某些特殊案件。第二，与胶州湾不同，旅顺港仅用作军港，仅供沙俄及中国舰船使用；而大连湾之港口一部分同旅顺港一样仅保留给中俄舰船使用，其他部分留作自由贸易港口供世界各国商船自由往来。第三，有关关东租借之条约明确规定有铁路特许经营权事项，而胶州湾之铁路特许经营权则另有协议规定。除需遵守关于中东线至大连湾延长线之建设协议规定外，中国还需严格执行1896年9月8日与俄中银行签订之协议。① 该协议具有商业及战略双重重大意义。除其他事项外，该协议还规定，经俄满铁路线由沙俄进口至中国或由中国出口至沙俄之货物，需分别缴纳进出口关税，税额较中国港口海关关税少三分之一。该协议初衷为发展中俄两国间贸易；应用于大连湾，也有利于沙俄在该港口之商业发展。然协议中最糟糕之规定来自第八条，规定俄满铁路及其附属设施之秩序及形象维护应交予俄军方指派之警务人员负责，并由俄方草拟及制订警察条例。此两项条约一旦实

---

① 俄满铁路协议全文见威尔的《重塑远东》，第2卷，第444页。

施，沙俄将成为租借地和铁路及其支线周围地区商业及军事主宰。第四，同年5月7日缔结之《中俄附加修正案（草案）》第五条规定，未经俄方同意，中国不得在中立区内铺设道路和开采矿产；而在胶州湾，其约束范围扩大至整个山东省。此外，协议规定未经俄方同意，中立区不得对其他势力做出让步；该规定并未出现在胶州湾相关条约中。最后一点不同之处在于，关东地区租期为25年，而非胶州湾之99年；关东租借协议并无租期届满前归还租借地之任何相关规定，仅规定在租期届满后经双方同意可延长租期。

沙俄治下之大连湾

正如前文所述，大连湾一部分按照条约规定仍用作自由贸易。沙俄虽更重视关东地区之军事及政治作用，但并没有忽视关东地区之商业重要性。维特先生计划把大连湾建成西伯利亚大铁路之商业终点口岸，并使其最终成为广袤俄罗斯帝国在太平洋上之商业出口地。日俄战争前，大连（大连湾）城市工程，包括其附属大型码头及普通码头，已耗资近2,000万卢布。[①]

因俄占时期大连湾只部分用作自由贸易港口，故而并无确切数据显示其商业增长。然而，俄国与东北间贸易往来可以大致说明大连湾之贸易状况：

日期	交易额（卢布）
1900	56,000,000
1901	51,000,000
1903	38,000,000

---

① 时卢布与美元汇率大约是1卢布兑换51美分。

第三章　关东

　　仅凭以上数据，似乎沙俄与东北贸易额在逐年减少；但实际上此一交易额下降系因沙俄从东北裁减军用运输额所致，而非沙俄商业运作不当。俄方租借关东地区后，即将大连湾部分留作自由贸易港，其实已经尽全力促进大连湾之贸易发展。俄方更通过降低运输资费以及免征大连湾关税等措施，极力将以往属于牛庄（原来列强在东北开展贸易之中心口岸）之贸易转移至俄国商人建立之港口。此外，俄方还采取措施增加本国对东北各地之进口总额。每年，沙俄派遣14艘商船在欧洲、海参崴、旅顺港及大连湾之间投入运营，每艘船只政府补贴309,000美元。① 由于俄中银行可向中国商人提供贷款，加之进口免关税及出口关税优惠等措施，美国领事米勒先生一再提醒沙俄有可能将主要由美国制造商掌控之东北棉花大贸易揽入怀中。② 有此商业顾虑，兼及其他政治因素，美国于1903年要求中国开放奉天【今沈阳】及安东【今丹东】，以供国际友人居住和往来贸易；日本在英美支持下，出于同样目的，要求开放大东沟，以削弱沙俄影响力。

　　关于该时期美国与东北之贸易，笔者尤有补充说明。此段时间，东北从美国进口商品超过从其他任何国家进口之商品；而自1900年至1904年，美国每年从牛庄进口约500万美元货物。③1901年，牛庄进口国内外商品总额为24,813,692美元，其中14,660,000美元为棉产品，其中约有1/3为美国布匹。1902年，牛庄35%进口货物来自美国，其中大部分是棉织品。1903年，外国进口总额为13,314,012美元，其中美国占5,562,255美元，其中4,873,960美元是棉织品。上述数字足以说明，此前几年，在东北最重要贸易品进口中，美国之地位举足轻重。尽管俄国人能生产出和美国商品几乎一样好之棉织品，但跨越西伯利亚5,000英里铁路线之运输费用两倍于跨越太平洋之运费。

―――――――
① 美国，《领事报告》，第73卷，第40页。
②《商业中国》，1904年，第2383页。
③《美国科学院年鉴》，第39—40卷，第157页。

因此，截至目前，进口床单、针织品及牛仔裤大部分仍来自美国。然美国之优势仅限于棉织品。自沙俄租借关东以来，源自美国之煤油及小麦面粉交易额持续下降。牛庄进口美国煤油从 1901 年之 317.2 万加仑下降至 1902 年的 603,180 加仑；而美国进口面粉也遭遇哈尔滨沙俄面粉工厂冲击，几乎被逐出市场。但此类物品仅占全部贸易一小部分，所以可以说，此一时期，尽管俄国人积极进取，大举挤占市场，美国人在东北的贸易状况依旧可观。

沙俄治下之旅顺港

有别于以贸易为主之大连湾，旅顺港纯系海军基地。沙俄加强了此港口之防御工事，令其成为重要之海军基地及军事要塞。从租借之初直至日俄战争，其间俄国在此共修建 59 座永久性要塞，包括著名之 203 高地以及尔灵山要塞与信号山要塞等；共安装大炮 546 门，其中包括 54 门大口径大炮；派驻大型战列舰 5 艘、炮艇 14 艘和小型船只 50 艘。由此可见，沙俄为建造旅顺港投入了巨大人力及物力。

条约规定之沙俄铁路经营特许权

条约规定，允许沙俄将中东铁路延伸至大连湾。为了理解此一延长线之重要性，不妨简要了解中东铁路之原貌。1896 年，俄中银行获得该铁路建设与开发权。东清铁路（中东铁路原称）主线全长 921 英里，[①]始于西伯利亚大铁路之满洲里，途经哈尔滨，终点为跨西伯利亚大铁路到海参崴之延伸点绥芬河。自哈尔滨开始之延伸工程全长 608 英里，其中包括长春至旅顺港 439 英里铁路线，后移交给日本，改称"南满铁路"。

[①]《中国年鉴》，1914 年，第 211 页、234 页。

第三章 关东

原条约规定，该铁路线归中东铁路公司所有，有效期为80年，期满后无偿归还中国。条约规定，在该线路投入运营36年后，中方方可以相当于线路成本加利息之价格赎回该线路。此规定亦适用于延长线。

中东铁路延长线建设进展迅速，至义和团运动爆发之时，除却几座桥梁外，几已全部竣工。义和团运动期间，大部分铁路线被毁，特别是从旅顺港到哈尔滨之延长线损毁尤为严重。即便如此，该项工程后来得以重启。1901年秋，中东铁路连同扩建工程全部竣工。全部工程耗资1.5亿美元，其中用于延长线建设金额为5,500万美元，此间费用并不涵盖用于旅顺港、大连和哈尔滨等城市建设以及严格而言不属于铁路建设之各相关企业建设所耗费之2.5亿卢布支出。

中东铁路对俄国而言意义重大，它将关东与满洲里、海参崴及哈尔滨（所谓"中国莫斯科"）相连接，然后经由跨西伯利亚大铁路抵到圣彼得堡，亦可经由（北）京奉（天）铁路到达北京。1909年5月，《远东评论》发表文章曰："该铁路系连接太平洋沿岸和西伯利亚大铁路之纽带，它贯穿中国境内之东北北部，并因此规避一条坎坷之道路，不必再沿着蜿蜒之黑龙江寻找出海口。与此同时，它亦提供了一条进占北京之新线路。"既如此，不止旅顺港落入沙俄手中，整个东北及中国之首都亦笼罩于沙俄军事威胁之阴影中。

最后，因修建铁路，沙俄获得铁路沿线及铁路线以外地区之采矿权以及护卫铁路之警察特权。虽则沙俄仅维护铁路就耗资高达2,400万卢布，约合1200万美元，但警察即士兵，士兵变警察，沙俄因此在中东铁路沿线拥有了一支宪兵部队，沙俄一旦有秘密任务，该宪兵部队便成为最具效率之行动队。

日俄冲突

世事多舛，奈何沙俄并非唯一垂涎关东之列强。沙俄来势汹汹，其对手亦咄咄逼人。沙俄力主将辽东半岛归还中国，旋即又借机将辽东半岛从中国手中租借走，日本对此难免耿耿于怀。

与沙俄相比，日本向上述领土扩张之意愿更为强烈。自 1828 年至日俄战争，日本人口几乎翻了一番。1828 年，日本人口仅 2,700 万；1875 年达到 3,400 万，1904 年更至 4,700 万。[①] 人口增长加剧了日本扩张之需求，亦成日俄利益冲突之重要因素。

此外，日本似乎以工业和贸易发展为主导方向，而非将农业发展摆在首位。当时日本耕地面积不足 1,300 万亩，仅占全国土地面积之 13%，其耕地面积无论如何增加亦无可能超过 1,050 万亩。显然，日本人均耕地份额甚至低于英国相应水平，不及中国之一半。佃户仅能勉强糊口，甚至无力支付必须之肥料，土地经营者利润亦难超 5%，却须支付所使用资本 15%~30% 之利息。此种情况下，日本人大多转向商贸一途。因此，1873 年，日本对外贸易额仅为 49,742,831 日元，但至 1903 年，已增至 606,637,959 日元。当此时，东北为列强在中国进行商业扩张最重要之场所，因此，为使日本贸易在东北市场蓬勃发展，日本势必要打开东北之大门。

最终，日本人便如其他野心勃勃之列强一样，给自身灌输了错误之民族意识。日本人认为，要成为世界强国，就必须不惜一切代价夺取他国领土。日本人相信伟大之日本应实现其对整个亚洲大陆之统治。帝国主义意味着大陆主义，而大陆主义必须通过军国主义来完成。

凡此种种，加之日本难以容忍沙俄侵占朝鲜和东北之行为，一场战争在所难免。日本似乎对沙俄归还辽东半岛未置一词，但如果看看以下资费用度，日本为战争所做之长期准备就会一目了然：

---

① K. Asakawa，《日俄冲突》，第 2 页。1910 年，日本人口增至 50,984,000 人。从 1904 年到 1910 年 6 年间，日本每年人口增长 70 万。

第三章 关东

日期	总支出（日元）	军费开支（日元）	%
1894–5	78,128,000	20,662,000	26.4
1895–6	85,317,000	23,536,000	27.6
1896–7	168,856,000	73,248,000	43.4
1897–8	223,678,000	110,542,000	49.3
1898–9	219,757,000	112,427,000	51.1
1899–0	254,165,000	114,212,000	44.9
1900–1	292,750,000	133,113,000	45.4
1901–2	266,856,000	102,360,000	38.3
1902–3	289,226,000	85,768,000	29.7
1903–4	244,752,000	71,368,000	31.7
1904–5	223,181,000	69,433,000	31.1

从上表可知，1896年后日本陆海军开支骤然增加；自1896年至1905年，日本陆海军平均支出占总支出40%。换言之，日本为日俄战争准备了足足九年！日本之备战概因战争是其控制关东唯一途径。战争可以为其打开通往东北之大门，此亦为最终实施其大陆战略之途径。而于沙俄一方而言，一与沙皇俄国以铁路线连通之不冻港如旅顺港及大连湾，亦为沙俄势力扩张之绝对必要条件。两国之重大利益系于一处，故两国均为战争做足了准备，均认为惟有战争方能解决争端。1904年2月8日晚，日俄战争爆发。

日本接手关东

本文无意讨论日俄战争。总而言之，战争至少暂时解决了领土争端以及其他问题。根据《朴次茅斯条约》，沙俄同意，如经中国应允，可将关东地区、铁路管理权及采矿权转让与日本。日本与中国随后召开会议。虽然会议对外并未报道有出现摩擦，但众所周知，中国极不情愿参与签订该条约，尤其抗拒其中关于将关东转让与日本之条款。中国希望废除此一耻辱条约，奈何心愿难成。1905 年 12 月 22 日，中国与日本缔结条约[①]，清政府同意沙俄根据条约中和平条款之第五条及第六条[②]，向日本进行一切权益之转移及委托。

日本治下之关东"政府"

1906 年 9 月 1 日，《日本帝国法令》颁布，规定关东"政府"及其下属机关之最高首脑为关东省省长，由日本驻军中拥有中将或大将衔之最高司令长官担任。总督管辖关东省，统率日本驻关东部队，并负责行政管理，由日本外务省节制。总督获特别许可权，可与中国地方当局谈判；且应在有关军事管理及人事事务上接受日本军政大臣、参谋总长及教育部军事监察长之节制。

转让后之旅顺港

前文数次提及旅顺港作为军事要塞及海军基地之重要性。"旅顺"二字日文写法与中文写法一致，发音类似"柳郡"，日本人将之作为日本关东军政当局总部。旅顺港分为新旧两部分。占领期间，日方设法修复俄国人建造之炮台及港口，并补足装备。1910 年 7 月 1 日[③]，名为促进国际贸易，实则为促进日本贸易，旅顺之西部港口开始向各国船只开放。大连—旅顺支线铁路开通之后，此两座港口间行程坐火车仅需 1.5 小时，愈加方便旅顺港军政当局采取措施，促进日本在大连之贸易。

[①] 赫茨莱特，《中国条约》，第 1 卷，第 392 页。
[②] 同上，第 610 页。第五条涉及关东租约的转让；第六条涉及长春—旅顺港铁路和煤矿的转让。
[③] 《中国年鉴与指南》，第 818 页。

第三章 关东

转让后之大连

"大连"之名称始用于移交之际,该港口旧称"大连湾"或"达里尼"。大连转由日本人租借之后最显著之特点,系日本利用其对该地区之政治及军事统治将一切有价值之物收入囊中,并设置法规将其竞争对手拒之门外。关于日本政府重视关东地区及东北贸易之新闻报道,米勒德先生撰文4篇,详加总结,要点如下:[①]

第一条:政府预付给在东北(及关东)经商日本商人提供总计600万日元的贷款担保,利率为4%,以帮助他们建立贸易关系或生产日本商品。

第二条:运往东北之日本货物,如符合一定之条件,可凭信用证交付。

第三条:"南满洲铁道株式会社"运送日本货物,免收运费,或按通常资费五折收费,为期一年。

第四条:日本商船载运本国货物至东北,免收海运费,或按通常资费一半收费,为期一年。

米勒德先生进而提到"不对从日本进口之日本商品征收关税"。

然而,此类不能一视同仁之措施并未长久持续,因为它导致驻北平各国外交使团敦促中国采取措施在大连设立中国海关。自1907年7月1日以来[②],大连港已形成一个海关区,其布局与胶州湾海关区相同。[③]大连是关东之总海关所在地,但并非关东地区唯一海关;锦州、普兰店、貔子窝(今皮口街)和旅顺港均设有海关。

大连为近代中国发展最快之口岸,其近年来之贸易额引人瞩目:

[①] 米勒德,《美国与远东问题》,第191页。
[②] 《中国年鉴》,1914,第120页。
[③] 参见本文第二章。此一安排消除了大连之关税歧视,但经由元山到达韩国之日本产品可经由千岛进入东北,仍无需缴纳关税,尽管此一路线运费颇高。

日期	进口（关制白银两）	出口（关制白银两）
1908	17,215,936	7,342,402
1909	12,239,563	22,318,144
1910	18,671,515	20,183,290
1911	24,012,724	24,184,154

由上表可知，大连之贸易非常繁荣，但繁荣仅属于日本。虽然德国、英国及比利时在大连之贸易额略有增加，但其他国家均受到严重影响，最糟糕者莫过于美国，其在该地区贸易额严重缩水。对比下表中日美进口额，可对具体情况有所了解[①]：

自1908年至1911年，关东从日本进口商品几近翻番，而从美国进口商品下降了93%以上。尽管1909年关东地区进口总额一度下降，然日本对该地区进口额却出人意料增长了20万两。[②]1911年，该地区超过四分之三之进出口贸易由日本人掌控。的确，相对廉价之劳动力、更为低廉之生产成本以及更低廉之运输成本有利于日本进口贸易。然而，威尔先生之言极具道理：考虑到铁路运输资费歧视以及日本常以火车需要修理而拖延其他国家货物运输时间等现状，东北实际上已成日本独家垄断之市场。

关东及东北人口研究

自1908年至1913年，仅过6年，东北南部日本人之人口几近翻番。此一汹涌之移民潮并非全然是人口自然流动之结果，亦为政策刺激下政府作为之成效。其间满洲日本人口数变化见下表[③]：

---

① 德意志商贸报告，1912年档案，第2部分，第642页。
② 参见本节第一处表格。
③ 《日本年鉴》，1914年，第713页、第39页。

第三章 关东

日期	日本人数量
1908	46,942
1909	53,906
1910	62,338
1912	73,568
1913	82,978

根据1913年所做的人口普查，日本在东北移民分布于以下各地[①]：

地点	日本人数量
关东	47,162
奉天	13,969
长春	6,208
安东（今丹东）	6,878
牛庄	6,358
哈尔滨	1,413
吉林 齐齐哈尔	990

如将关东地区两座主要城市——大连及旅顺港——之中日人口加以对比，对于日本向该地区移民之凶猛自会有更清晰认识[②]：

地点	日本人	中国人
大连	29,395	20,338
旅顺港	9,637	8,222

除旅顺港、大连及哈尔滨等地俄国人一度占据人口大多数外，笔者在中国其他地方还未曾发现有外国人超过中国人之现象。

---

① 《日本年鉴》，1914年，第713页、第38页。
② 《日本年鉴》，1914年，第713页。

日本人源源不断涌入中国既有经济追求，亦有政治目的，然其社会影响远超政治经济范畴，甚至动摇了中国社会之伦理纲常。米勒德先生援引英国传教士语称："日本移民之行为表现令人大失所望……成千上万之日本男人与道德败坏之女性在城市及乡镇大街上行猥琐乃至苟且之事，于此一腐朽没落之国家——至少在一定程度上——又添一衰败印象。"[1] 当然，应该看到，此一说法难免有以偏概全之嫌，至少就私生活而言，许多日本移民尚能洁身自好。

关东之经济状况

仅凭数据，关东地区财政预算极易误导对关东经济之印象。此财政预算既不包括军事开支，也不包括南满铁道株式会社利润，而此两项恰恰构成关东财政状况之要素。[2]

关东财政一般收入来自税收、公共事业、国有财产、印花税和杂项收入。公共事业及国有财产系普通收入中最大项目，据估计为1,626,000日元，占1914—1915年预算中普通收入总额五分之四以上。特别财政收入主要为出售国有财产所得及中央财政拨款。第一种收入主要指俄国人转让以及从中方购买之土地。属于南满洲铁道株式会社之土地总面积（包括其在东北及关东之土地）为70.54平方英里（45,156英亩）。关东每年公共土地买卖情况如右：

日期	价值（日元）
1908—1909	1,200
1909—1910	1,200
1910—1911	17,616
1911—1912	18,000
1912—1913	777,000
1913—1914	10,000
1914—1915	26,000

---

[1] 米勒德：《美国与远东问题》，第222页。
[2] 《日本年鉴》，1908—1909年，第573页；1910年，第633页；1912年，第662页；1913年，第683页；1914年，第714页。

第三章　关东

每年财政部补助金从 2,307,000 日元增加到 3,964,000 日元。根据 1914 年至 1915 年预算，总收入达到了 443.7 万日元。

至于开支，1914—1915 年度预算中最大开支项系交通费，计 105 万日元；警察和监狱费用为 91 万日元，尚有其他各项开销，总支出共计 443.7 万日元。

笔者想要明确之一点是，收入 443.7 万日元而支出亦为 443.7 万日元，这显然并非真实财务状况之反映。

1913—1914 年度关东及"满洲"水域海军支出耗费日本 96.6 万日元，而该地区驻扎之陆军费用为 466 万日元。如此一来，日本在该地区一年军费支出高达 550 万日元，实为一笔数额不菲之开支。

556.6 万日元军费开支由日本政府全额支付，加上同年（1913—1914）之财政部拨款，总支出竟至 8,674,000 日元。当时日本国库并不富足，怎有可能年复一年支付如此高昂之开支？日本人手里没能存有资本，但日本人拥有一台可以制造资本之机器，此机器即为南满洲铁道株式会社（简称"满铁"）。满铁 1913—1914 财政年度净利润为 7,167,000 日元，这笔款项几乎可以承担日本在关东及东北地区当年度所有支出。日本人希望满铁收益可以逐年增加，期待可以此抵销政府支出。诚然，满铁公司利润并非全部用于支付政府股息；但无可否认，满铁公司由日本政府兴办，公司管理层由政府任命，公司利润自然需要充入国库而非增加私人股东收益。同时必须明确，东北地区之陆海军绝非仅为保护关东而存在，满铁负责之范围亦不限于关东，而涵盖东北南部全域事务。事实上，日本操控东北是为了控制关东，而控制关东地区则又是为了进一步操控东北；两地财政盘根错节，难分彼此，如欲撇开一地财政而考察另一地之财政状况绝无可能。故而将关东与东北地区实际财政收支合并开列下表：

一、收入

日期	总收入（日元）	拨款（日元）	满铁净利润（日元）
1907—1908	4,386,000	3,000,000	1,087,988
1908—1909	4,653,602	3,120,000	7,375,734
1909—1910	4,653,489	3,964,000	
1910—1911	4,867,988	3,615,000	7,161,000
1911—1912	4,984,926	3,643,000	4,928,000
1912—1913	5,246,000	3,122,000	4,926,000
1913—1914	5,739,000	3,047,000	7,167,000
1914—1915	4,437,000	2,307,000	

二、开支

日期	总支出（日元）	驻军支出（日元）	海军支出（日元）
1907—1908	4,386,293		
1908—1909	4,653,802		
1909—1910	4,879,489	5,713,000	1,115,000
1910—1911	4,867,988	5,296,000	1,091,000
1911—1912	4,984,926	5,009,000	1,167,000
1912—1913	5,246,000	4,497,000	1,095,000
1913—1914	5,697,000	4,660,000	966,000
1914—1915	4,437,000		

南满洲铁道株式会社

经中国政府同意,沙俄将长春、大连及旅顺口段之南满铁路移交给日本政府①,日本天皇敕令组建南满洲铁道株式会社,对该地区之铁路实施运营。1906年6月,满铁正式宣布成立。满铁筹委会于1906年8月10日举行第一次会议。时人认为此乃具有国家性质之私营公司。1907年4月1日,铁路现场办公会决议正式将南满铁路及其所有产权转让给满铁公司。1908年7月,南满铁路管理权移交日本交通省,嗣后移交帝国铁道董事会。

在股份分配一事上,满铁筹委会于1906年第一次大会上确定将满铁股份化,共计2亿日元,其中日本政府占1亿日元,包括(1)已建成之铁路②,(2)上述铁路附属之不动产③,(3)抚顺及烟台两处煤矿④。其余股份提供给日本及中国有意向之股东。然而,中国人未能利用此一机会购买满铁股份。⑤1908年,满铁在欧洲筹集到800万英镑贷款,而诸股东实际支付资金仅200万日元。1911年1月,满铁在伦敦筹得6,000万日元外国贷款,其中2,000万日元用于偿还短期贷款,其余部分用于重建安奉铁路(今丹东—沈阳线)。⑥令人意外之处乃日本人善于吸纳外资发家致富。为了争取投资,日本政府向投资人确保其利润不低于6%。⑦

此乃南满州铁道株式会社之历史及股份化过程。如是,其惟铁路公司乎?

---

① 交接于1906年8月1日进行。
② 不包括正在使用的铁路库存,沈阳轻轨及其相关设施。
③ 不包括租借区内的不动产。
④ 《远东评论》,1909年11月刊,第288页。
⑤ 同上,第289页。
⑥ 《日本年鉴》,1912年,第664页。
⑦ 同上,第669页。

以其行政管理体制而言，除股东大会选举之审计师外，其余高层管理人员均由政府任命。审计师任期3年，总裁、副总裁任期5年，董事任期4年。尽管政府须从至少拥有50股以上股东中挑选总裁、副总裁与董事，但除却此项限制，政府乃公司惟一控制人。从公司与中央政府关系来看，满铁不仅是一家商业公司，而且还是政府代理人。

就其履行职能而言，满铁不仅控制铁路，其亦涉足其他各种业务，采矿、海运、港务、仓储、电力和煤气工程等，无所不能。满铁主要以自己之铁路运输并销售货物；享有在其铁路沿线建造和管理房产之权利；有权在其铁路沿线提供经费，从事教育、卫生和工程等基础建设。满铁甚至还被委托向辖区内居民、收取赋税，以支付上述之公益事业资费。因此，从公司性质及权力范围来看，满铁已不仅仅是一家铁路公司，更是租借地之管理者。除了关东"政府"监管之治安权，日本领事拥有之司法权之外，满铁在其辖区内可以说无所不能。

在关东境内以及连接关东之日本铁路

在关东境内以及连接关东且由满铁直接控制之日本铁路线有两条：（1）由沙俄转让而来之长春—大连线及其支线，（2）经中日协议交与日本控制之安奉线（今丹东—沈阳铁路）。此外，还有另两条不归满铁管理之铁路，一条名为"长春—吉林铁路"，另一条名为"新民屯—沈阳铁路"。铁路修建资本一半是从日本借贷而来，但铁路控制权掌握在中国人手中。

1913年底，日本亦曾尝试采取其他措施在东北南部构建铁路网。

长春—大连铁路线系由俄罗斯转交给日本，全长439.5英里，于1907年通车。除439.5英里之主干线外，该铁路线尚有诸多支线：其一为苏家屯—抚顺煤矿线，全长 34.5 英里；其二为大石桥—营口线，全长 13.5 英里；其三为周水子—旅顺港线，长 31.5 英里。此一主干线及各支线均属标准轨距之铁路线，对此一主干线及各支线之运营管理概以 1896 年中国与俄中银行达成之原始协议为基准。自中东铁路运营之日起 80 年为期，满铁对该线路享有所有权，期满后无偿归还中国。倘中国有意于租期届满前赎回该铁路线，可在该线路投入运营 36 年后出资购买，价格相当于该线路之建设成本及其利息。

安奉铁路为应对日俄战争需要临时修建，工程粗糙。之后，根据 1905 年 12 月 22 日日中签订之附加条约第六款[①]，日本获得修缮并运营安奉铁路之特权，从条约签订之日起，为期 15 年。租期届满后，中国政府可以市场估价或仲裁裁定之价格赎回该铁路线。然而，日本人视"修缮"为"重建"，故意更改铁路线路及轨距。此一做法既有违条约，亦有违门户开放原则。雷亚先生尝言："关键是，竟无任何国家对日本之行径提出正式抗议。英美两国自诩为最遵守门户开放原则之国家，然此处对日本之默许及纵容何其明显。"[②]

安奉铁路全长 162 英里，1906 年 12 月移交给满铁，之前一直由日本军方控制。1908 年 8 月安奉铁路建成通车。[③] 1908 年 11 月 11 日，安奉线调整为宽轨距线路。

以上两条铁路线及其支线总长 701 英里，横贯当今世界最富饶地区之一。它们将朝鲜、西伯利亚和中国华北连通在一起，真正令日本成为该地区之主导势力。

在此，不妨简要了解美国对日俄在东北之铁路建设及相关管理制度所持态度。由于中东铁路和"南满"铁路严重威胁未来美国在华利益，1910 年，美国建议将此二条铁路中立化。但由于遭到日俄强烈反对，

---

① 赫茨莱特，《中国条约》，第 1 卷，第 395 页。
② 《远东评论》，1909 年 11 月，第 295 页。
③ 同上，第 296 页。

该计划未能实施。

目前尚未讨论之第三条及第四条铁路线分别为长春—吉林铁路和新民屯—沈阳铁路,长春至吉林铁路线长80英里。此二条线路虽由中国政府直接控制,但常受日本人左右。如欲分清个中原委,还需对其深入了解。

1907年以前,新民屯—沈阳铁路由日本人运营。由于该铁路为北京—沈阳铁路线之一段,因此,中国能否控制此一铁路意义重大。1907年4月15日[①],中日签署条约,中国政府以199万日元价格购买新民屯—沈阳铁路,条件如下:

(一)中国政府在修建辽东铁路(新民屯—沈阳段)及长春至吉林铁路时,所需款项之一半应从满铁筹借。贷款期限分别为:新民屯—沈阳线18年,吉林—长春线25年。[②]

(二)日后修建长春—吉林铁路支线时,如遇资金不足之情况,中国须向日本借贷,不留他国与日本竞争之机会。

(三)借贷期间,应由日本人担任铁路总工程师及会计师。

(四)以上各铁路收入应存入日本银行。

(五)中国修建之新民屯—沈阳铁路线以及长春—吉林铁路线都需与"南满铁路"连接。

东北之采矿业

重要性仅次于铁路特许经营权者乃矿业开采权。开采中国矿产资源不仅有利于增加年收入,亦有利于列强巩固其在华势力范围。

抚顺煤矿[③]位于沈阳以东约22英里处,含有厚度为80至175英

---

① 赫茨莱特,《中国条约》,第1卷,第397页。
② 贷款偿还期限自铁路通车之日起算,即1912年10月20日。
③ 《日本年鉴》,1913年,第688页;1914年,第716页。

尺之矿床，煤炭储量估计至少为 8 亿吨。当前该矿已有数个矿井同时开挖，日产总计 3000 吨。

烟台煤田位于辽阳北部，从烟台火车站坐火车一小时即可到达，日产原煤达 100 吨。

抚顺及烟台煤矿预计煤炭年产量如下表所示：

日期	产出（吨）	净利润（日元）
1911	1,382,000	2,628,000
1912	1,513,000	1,846,000
1913	2,281,000	1,800,000

为方便原煤运输，两座煤矿均已建成铁路支线，以连接煤矿和"南满铁路"。抚顺支线长 38.9 英里，烟台支线长 9.7 英里。1908 年，两条支线均告通车。

1904 年后沙俄在东北之影响

的确，日本在满洲之扩张系以挤占沙俄之势力为代价，然沙俄于此间之影响是否因日俄战争之战败而消失？沙俄是否已丧失争夺之念？然，事实上，沙俄仍然影响着三分之二之东北地区，包括整个东北北部地区，涵盖松花江及其支流流经地区。沙俄与东北共同控制着汹涌之黑龙江；并在符拉迪沃斯托克（海参崴）建立起坚固港口，该港口通过满铁以及跨西伯利亚大铁路与西伯利亚以及位于沙皇俄国之欧洲领土相连；沙俄对蒙古之控制并无实质性削弱，帝国阴影一直笼罩着蒙古。沙俄在东北之地位系由《朴次茅斯条约》确定，于国际范围内享有与日本相同之权益。"北满"铁路仍由俄国警卫监管。在东北附近之齐齐哈尔、蒙加尔、艾根、桑桑、乌尔加等地方均有俄国驻军。

虽则俄罗斯政策力度不如日本，然日俄战争后至 1908 年间，沙俄来东北移民数量增加了 2 倍：1906 年为 18 万，1907 年为 40 万，1908 年为 50 万。

沙俄在东北拥有 8 家面粉厂，日产量达 47,000 普特。为提供军事补给及应对意外情况，沙俄已做好充分准备。① 显然，沙俄并没有忘记 1904 年战争之耻辱；日本亦没有对沙俄之秘密计划掉以轻心。因此，米勒德先生尝言："一更强大之日本将无异于为沙俄东方政策敲响丧钟；而沙俄在华势力之壮大则意味着日本最终无法获得在华之霸权。面对列强，中国惟有依靠自己，解决纠纷，才有可能维持远东国际势力均衡。"

---

① 俄罗斯位于东北的面粉厂如下所示：

地点	日产量（普特）
松花江制粉厂	10,000
佐祖林斯基制粉厂	7,000
东北制粉公司	6,000
德鲁赞制粉厂	2,000
里夫制粉厂	3,000
诺瓦尔斯基制粉厂	7,000
图尔金制粉厂	10,000
克朗丁诺夫制粉厂	1,000

第四章

广州湾

第四章 广州湾

广州湾（法文正式拼写为 Kouang-Tchéou-Wan）为法国租借地，距香港 230 英里，位于广东省海岸线上。① 1899 年新增两座岛屿，总面积 190 平方英里。② 条约于 1898 年 5 月 27 日由中法双方签订，性质与中德两国签订之胶州湾租借条约一致。③

广州湾之行政管理

1899 年 11 月 6 日，广西提督苏元春与法国海军准将高礼睿签署中法广州湾租借地条约，将广州湾归入法属印度支那联邦总督辖下。④ 该租借地计有 3 个行政区域，然中国原有公共管理机构得以保留。⑤

港口城市巴亚尔堡

广州湾首府巴亚尔堡，位于檀尾河右岸入海口处，为广州湾租借地之商业中心。广州湾被视作自由贸易港，湾内所有商业活动均享有免税特惠。"杜纳总督希望借由豁免关税及特许进出商船自由航行促使广州湾不日成为远东主要转运港之一。"⑥ 广州湾商贸随后确实发展迅速。1912 年，广州湾进出口贸易额约 8,412,875 越币⑦，合 3,600,000 美元。

---

① 《中国行业名录及记事》，1914 年，第 1082 页。
② 《政治家年刊》，1906 年，第 877 页。
③ 赫茨莱特，《中国条约》，第 328 页。
④ 法属印度支那联邦下辖五个邦，曰安南、柬埔寨、交趾支那、东京及老挝。整个法属印度支那联邦设一总督，统一管理联邦事务，并设秘书长一名协理政务。除交趾支那外，每邦均设有行政首脑一名，曰行政公使；总督兼领交趾支那行政首脑。
⑤ 《政治家年刊》，1914 年，第 851 页。
⑥ 雷纳齐，《殖民管理》，第 245—246 页。
⑦ 《政治家年刊》，1906 年，第 849 页。1 个越币约合 0.428 美元。

广州湾海军基地

海湾入口处有硇洲岛及东海岛，令广州湾成为极佳之封闭型港口，仅可沿两条狭窄通道进入湾内。正如莫尔斯先生所言，"广州湾系绝佳之锚地，然很难通过沙岸。"[①] 基地兵营建在檀尾河畔。总体而言，五个海军基地中，广州湾最无军事价值。

广州湾之财政

关于广州湾之财务状况，笔者手头并无确切数据。仅知 1914 年广州湾地方财政预算为 32.3 万越币，约合 15 万美元，与威海卫年度预算相当。

《广州湾租借地条约》授予之铁路特许权

中法《广州湾租借地条约》授予法国特许铁路建设权，法国政府旋即委托印度支那铁路建设公司承担该项工作。1910 年，老街至云南铁路线通车，全长约 287 英里。此一铁路线与全长 248 英里之老街—海防铁路线相连接，就此将云南府与海岸连通，并有可能令海防港成为中国西南部货物出口之重要口岸。原本法国征服东京【附属印度支那联邦之一，今天越南的一部分——译者注】之目的即为通过云南府同中国建立商业及政治互通关系。此亦法国耗费巨大精力修建东京—云南府铁路线之原因。[②] 法国工程师决心既定，克服了从红河水面到云南高原 1,600 米之海拔落差；法国金融家为此不惜投入了

---

① 莫尔斯，《中国贸易与管理》，第 268 页。
② 《远东评论》，1909 年 11 月刊，第 303 页。

第四章　广州湾

32,216,000 美元总成本，抑或说平均每英里铁路线 6 万美元之代价。①后法国往印度支那增兵，引起清政府外交衙门警惕，质疑法国此举之目的。随后外交衙门与法国外交部长谈判达成明确协议，规定中国及法国均不得在云南—东京铁路沿线派驻军队，且铁路之中国段应由中国警察看守。1909 年，清政府外交衙门电令云南总督要求就地操练士兵，以备不虞。广州湾系因商业考虑而租借给外国之另一事例，实可谓后患无穷；然其最初之商业考虑竟是为"巩固与法国之友谊"。

广州湾租借地之主要特征

德国首相俾斯麦曾就英德法三国之殖民事务作如下总结："英格兰既有殖民地，亦有殖民者；德国有殖民者，但无殖民地；法国有殖民地，但无殖民者。"广州湾与印度支那联邦之殖民统治之状况确曾如此。尽管道默先生锐意改革，大力加强印度支那联邦及广州湾之行政管理，该租借地之殖民者人口密度仍很稀薄。

---

① 《远东评论》，1909 年 11 月刊，第 304 页。

第五章

威海卫

第五章　威海卫

威海卫乃英国租借地，地处北纬37.30度，东经122.10度，位于山东半岛东北海岸。威海卫租借地包括刘公岛及威海卫湾内所有岛屿和海湾沿岸10英里地方，总面积为285平方英里，尚不包括1,505平方英里之中立区。1898年7月1日，中英双方在北京签署《订租威海卫专条》（简称《专条》），正式将威海卫租与英国。①

邓比曾表示②，就其地理位置而言，"威海卫乃绝佳之港口，较之旅顺港大且优良。"③威海卫正处渤海湾之入海口，为湾上距朝鲜最近之处，扼制全湾。威海卫距烟台40英里，胶州湾80英里，极有可能成为第二个香港或华北之香港。"④

就其战略重要性而言，查尔斯·贝雷斯福德认为"此为我海军力量在中国海域之巨大收获，只需些微开支，即可建成强力高效之海军基地。"⑤他又补充道："当前在中国海域，尚无其他港口可允准战舰如此靠近海岸。"⑥然，贝雷斯福德亦坦言，就当时（1898年）情况而言，威海卫之战略地位尚无法与旅顺港相提并论。

威海卫航运便利，有利商贸；然，铁路设施薄弱，尚难成就上佳之商业港口。

英国强租威海卫之过程⑦

既然未能说服俄国放弃租借旅顺港及大连湾，且感觉俄国之旅大租借地与德国之胶州湾租借地威胁英国在华北之商业利益，1898年3

---

① 赫茨莱特，《中国条约》，第1卷，第122页。
② 《美国总统咨文和外交关系》，1898年，第190页。
③ 但是这一点优势实际并没有显现出来。
④ 还有待时间才能实现。
⑤ 查尔斯·贝雷斯福德，《瓜分中国》，第71页。
⑥ 同上，第72页。
⑦ 《日本每周邮报》，1898年。

月 25 日，英国决议尽快租借威海卫。4 月 3 日，驻香港英国舰队奉命前往渤海湾。诸公须知，自中日甲午战争日军攻陷威海卫至此一时间，日本人长期盘踞于此。但有可能，日本人自不会放弃继续控制威海卫之野心。然受俄罗斯及德国在中国北方海域夹击，日本孤立无援，无计可施。日本对英国租借威海卫未置一词，表面上未有异议，实则居心叵测，欲与英国结盟，共御强敌。于是威海卫之领土租借交接顺利完成，随后威海卫归由英国海军部兼理。

威海卫之行政管理[①]

1898 年英国占据威海卫后，租借地行政管理由驻防该地的英国海军将领担任，次年移交给由陆军部任命的军事及民事长官。1901 年 1 月 1 日，威海卫划归英国殖民署直接管理。1902 年，殖民署正式任命一名行政长官，负责威海卫行政长事务。

最高行政长官之任命需有英国国王签名盖章。根据 1901 年 7 月 24 日之《【枢密院】威海卫法令》，行政长官有权制定法令，但须经殖民事务大臣批准。为加强管理，该法令规定在威海卫设立高等法院，高等法院具有一应民事及刑事管辖权，亦可向香港最高法院上诉。此外，法令亦规定设立地区治安法院。

村社则按照中国习俗交由村长管理。

条约内容[②]

1898 年 7 月 1 日，中英双方签订《订租威海卫专条》。条约规定，

---

① 《殖民办公室列表》，1914 年，第 401 页；《中国行业名录和记事》，第 829 页。
② 赫茨莱特，《中国条约》，第 1 卷，第 122 页。

在租借地范围（285平方英里）内，英国拥有唯一管辖权；中国官员仍可在城内各司其事，惟不得对保卫租借地之英军有所妨碍。

至于1,505平方英里之中立区，仍由中国管辖治理，英国不予干预；除中英两国兵卒外，他国军队不得擅入。

《专条》第一款规定，英国对威海卫之租期应与俄国租借旅顺之期相同。尽管旅顺港已于1905年1月1日落入日本之手，英国却无任何撤出威海卫之意向，且另与中国达成一项新协议，准允英国保留租期25年，从《中俄条约》签署之日起算。

爱德华港

威海卫租借地主要港口为爱德华港，因纪念爱德华七世加冕而得名。爱德华港为自由贸易港口，主要开展帆船和轮船贸易。1912年，计有总载重524,927吨、632艘轮船进出该港，其中452艘为英国船只，180艘为日本和中国沿海小船。[①] 此数据虽不涵盖海军部运煤舰船以及政府公务用船，然已可见此港口作为自由贸易港难成大器。

海军基地威海卫[②]

虽有邓比和贝雷斯福德对威海卫海军基地之高度评价，然该基地军事防御能力并不稳固。一则因有英日同盟之存在，便如众人之见，同盟之下已无加固基地防御之必要；二则因英国无意承担防御工事所需之巨大开支。如今威海卫已成为英国海军飞行基地及补给站，属英国海军"中国舰队"之训练基地及疗养站；该舰队由50艘舰船组成，

---

① 《政治家年刊》，1914年，第180页。
② 同上，第179页。

于夏季在威海卫海面集结。英国于威海卫陆地并无驻军，英军之"中国军团"早已解散。1899 年，英国于当地军务耗资 13 万英镑；此后英国再无此项军费开支。

威海卫之财政状况分析

威海卫财政收入包括地税、路税、船只登记费、船务费、酒类消费税、罚款及其他杂项收入。政府收入只占开支一半多一点，因此，威海卫财政收支尚不能自给自足。该财政赤字靠英国政府拨款填补，然数额不大，较之德国对胶州湾及日本对关东之拨款可谓微不足道。威海卫之年度收入、支出及政府拨款如下表所示[①]：

日期	收入	开支	拨款（英镑）
1901—1902			11,250
1902—1903			12,000
1903—1904	58,364	166,921	9,000
1904—1905	90,415	162,282	6,000
1905—1906	105,934	146,120	3,000
1906—1907	76,777	160,973	4,000
1907—1908	80,331	173,341	10,000
1908—1909	83,277	168,740	10,000
1909—1910	83,499	145,687	4,000
1910—1911	75,353	145,028	5,000
1911—1912	14,673	153,591	6,000
1912—1913	79,582	146,147	6,000
1913—1914	72,436		8,300

---

① 1903—1913 年的数字源自《殖民办公室列表》，1914 年，第 401 页；1901—1903 的数字源自《政治家年刊》，1906 年，第 195 页；1913—1914 的数字源自《政治家年刊》，1914 年，第 179 页。

采矿业及铁路

威海卫没有发展采矿业,也没有修建铁路。该租借地曾有金矿,一家采矿公司平稳运营两年之后,现已停止经营。[1] 在德国占领胶州湾初期,英国与德国达成外交协议,同意不在山东省享有任何铁路特许权,以避免事态复杂化。英国在威海卫遵守了该项行政协议。

威海卫于英国之重要性

众所周知,列强中英国与中国贸易量最大。英国进占威海卫之前,中国北部沿海 3 个主要港口为烟台、天津及牛庄。根据 1897 年统计数据[2],此 3 个港口清关之货物总计 4,042,928 吨,其中 2,265,658 吨系由英国船只运载。1897 年此 3 个港口贸易总额为 103,469,664 两银子[3],其中一半以上系与英国人交易所得。当时英国仅与东北之贸易额即超过 300 万英镑。1897 年在渤海湾 3 个港口进出船只吨位分布如下[4]:

港口	清关货物总吨位	英国清关货物吨位
烟台	2,385,301	1,327,559
牛庄	730,964	363,922
天津	1,326,663	574,177
总计	4,042,928	2,265,658

此乃 1897 年英国强租威海卫数月前其在渤海湾之贸易状况。如此一海域英国不设海军基地,则英国商船将任由俄国和德国宰割。威

---

[1] 《政治家年刊》,1906 年,第 195 页。
[2] 《美国商业关系》,1898 年和 1899 年,第 1 卷,烟台、牛庄和天津数据。
[3] 1897 年,1 两银子约合 0.75 美元。
[4] 查尔斯·贝雷斯福德,《瓜分中国》,附录,第 484 页。

海卫作为海军基地对英国而言意义重大，因为英国人视其为自身在中国北方贸易之惟一保障。

威海卫之未来

英国以保护自身在华商业利益不受俄国侵占关东及德国占领胶州湾影响为由，强行租借威海卫。1914年11月，关东及胶州湾相继落入与英国有同盟关系之日本之手，英国遂放弃威海卫之防御工事，概因英国认定英日同盟已使威海卫之防御工事无存之必要。单从理论上讲，确有可能如此，日本既已掌控关东及胶州湾，英国已不需要威海卫为其商船之保障。据此，租期届满，英国自然应将威海卫归还中国。但事实果真如此乎？英国在中国海域之敌人会随着关东及胶州湾之陷落而消失乎？英日会永结同盟乎？威海卫之未来命运很大程度上取决于此等问题之答案。

日本在各方面都与英国有相似之处：日本与英国均系岛国，日本与英国均系海军强国，日本与英国均系制造业国家。两国有着同样之需求，同样之供给，同样之野心及争夺目标。此二国携手同盟只不过是权宜之计，故而无须对此深入探究，吾等只需好生回顾其为在中国之商业霸主地位你争我夺之历史即可。

1909年，英国对中国出口棉纺织品占中国进口棉纺织品总量10/16；然至1910—1912年间，其占比大幅下降。尽管在1913年有所回升，其占比亦仅为9/16。1913年，日本对中国出口棉纺织品占中国进口棉纺织品总量从1/16增长至5/16。① 得益于其廉价劳动力及近

---

① 棉制品名目下，笔者仅计入衬衫、床单、针织衫、牛仔裤和T恤等。日本与英国棉制品出口中国情况如右：

年份	英国（件）	日本（件）
1909	10,691,448	1,396,297
1910	6,511,126	2,389,693
1911	11,317,630	2,832,625
1912	9,618,386	3,043,747
1913	11,705,426	5,716,594

水楼台之便，日本相较英国之对中国出口贸易优势日益明显。日英之间商业竞争几乎覆盖商业贸易之各行各业，其中棉纺织品贸易尤为突出。威尔先生曾言："概因英美诸国施以舆论及经费援助，终致日本在日俄战争中胜出；然俄国虽败，势力犹存，日本惟有竭力在中国沿海地区扩张势力范围并从东亚之中立区获取赔偿，非遇英美诸国势力集结之地域而不罢休，终致日本成为在华势力范围之第一国。"① 大多数英国人都对日本人缺乏信任，即便未曾去过远东之英国人亦抱此种态度。英国人对所谓英日同盟深表怀疑，事实上英国人从不看好英日同盟。英国租借威海卫，意在借此与俄德在华势力抗衡。对于俄德两国在渤海湾失势，英国人不免内心窃喜。不曾想前门拒虎后门进狼，此时保有威海卫租借地对英日关系影响尤为重大。

至于中国北部沿海贸易状况，根据1911年及1912年有关数据记载，英国在中国天津、烟台、胶州及牛庄诸港口贸易额达11,000,000英镑，占诸港口贸易额总量之40%。1911年天津港国外净进口总额为7,098,768英镑，其中1,108,164英镑来自英国②；1912年牛庄总进口额为21,280,721英镑，其中453,518英镑来自英国③；1911年胶州湾总贸易额为6,995,866英镑，其中发往欧洲之货物，超过60%流向英国④；1912年烟台港进口总额为672,353英镑，其中276,615英镑为英国人所有⑤。总而言之，英国在中国北部沿海之商业贸易实可谓独占鳌头⑥，然英国人在以上港口之贸易安全，很大程度有赖于英国驻威海卫海军力量之保障，此一事实在随后几年直接决定了威海卫之命运。

---

① 威尔，《即将到来之东亚斗争》，第519页。
② 《下议院会期文档》，1912—1913年，第94卷，第4902号文档。
③ 同上，第4901号文档。
④ 同上，第95卷，第4935号文档。
⑤ 同上，1912年，第95卷，第5071号文档。
⑥ 唯一例外为大连湾之贸易额构成，根据1912年统计数据，英国货物进口额（包括中国香港）仅占大连湾贸易额总量之6%，而同期日本货物进口额占比高达71.5%。

第六章

九龙（新界）

第六章 九龙新界

九龙为又一英国租借地,位于已"割让"之香港附近。九龙面积为 366 平方英里,其中陆地面积 286 平方英里,岛屿面积近 90 平方英里。① 九龙指九龙半岛北部从大鹏湾到深圳湾大片土地以及邻近之岛屿(含老岛),系 1898 年 6 月 9 日租借给英国。②

九龙不仅地理位置重要,且于香港意义非同小可。就其本身而言,大鹏湾、深圳湾、青山湾及吐露港均为上佳海军基地;有铁路与内地连通,堪称交通要道。相对香港而言,其对香港之保护,犹如头骨之保护大脑一般。九龙既是香港之腹地,亦为香港之屏障。如欲清楚认识九龙之重要性,必先了解香港之重要性。

言及香港之地理位置,香港中华总商会有一款章程曰:"香港地处印度与日本之间,毗邻广东(中国人口最多省份之一),为亚洲最发达内陆水运网之出海口,于英国贸易至关重要。"

言及香港贸易,总商会指出:"香港之贸易,今(1898 年)粗略估计每年约有 5,000 万英镑,待华南河道开放,长江流域铁路建成,预计香港贸易仍将大幅增长。"就世界范围航运而言,今日之香港亦为世界最大航运中心之一。世界各大港口具体吞吐吨位如下③:

城市	进出吞吐吨位(吨)
纽约(1912)	13,673,763
安特卫普(1911)	13,330,699
香港(1912)	12,100,365
汉堡(1911)	11,830,949
鹿特丹(1911)	11,052,186
上海(1911)	9,429,996
伦敦(1911)	9,004,974

---

① 《中国行业名录和记事》,1914 年,第 1108 页。
② 赫茨莱特《中国条约》,第 1 卷,第 120 页。
③ 《统计摘要》,1912 年,第 815 页。

1913 年有数据记载①，英国自香港贸易进口金额为 676,293 英镑，而其对香港出口额高达 4,358,902 英镑，占香港贸易额五成。

此乃香港之贸易概况。香港中华总商会宣称："无论英国之华中贸易重要性几何，诸君须谨记，其在远东影响力及威望仍系于香港。"

于英国在华势力范围之影响，香港亦至关重要。香港中华总商会章程第二款对此归纳如下：

> 香港通过铁路线，先连通广东，最终连通汉口及其姊妹城市武昌和汉阳，势力范围直达中国商业之核心腹地。

正是香港令九龙新界变得尤为重要；也正是香港，促使英国选定九龙新界而非其他地方作为租借地。

行政管理

九龙新界实施乡村社区管理制度，由香港政府直接辖制。② 新界行政公署设在大鹏湾狭长处之大埔湖，设行政长官一人，履行警事及治安法官职责。新界南区交由助理行政长官管理。条约有文规定③，在九龙新城内，当时驻扎于此地之中国官员可继续行使管辖权，但不可与保卫香港之军务相冲突【条约原文为："又议定，所有现在九龙城内驻扎之中国官员，仍可在城内各司其事，惟不得与保卫香港之武备有所妨碍。"——译者注】。至 1899 年，九龙新城内中国官员停

---

① 《政治家年刊》，1914 年，第 118 页。
② 香港行政由总督主理，行政局协理。行政局除总督外，有 6 名官守议员及 2 名非官守议员。立法局亦由总督主理，其中 3 名由总督推荐并经英王提名（通常有 2 人为华人，1 人从太平绅士中选出，另 1 人由华人商会提名）。香港法制以英国普通法为基础，辅以殖民地地方法令加以修正。参见《殖民办公室列表》，1914 年，第 211 页。
③ 赫茨莱特，《中国条约》，第 1 卷，第 120 页。

第六章　九龙新界

止行使管辖权；随后，根据英国枢密院令，九龙新城并入租借地，由英国统治。①

协议条款②

1898年6月9日于北京签订之《展拓香港界址专条》与《威海卫条约》颇多相似之处，亦有两点不同。首先，九龙新界租期为99年，而威海卫为25年。其次，须注意，《展拓香港界址专条》中有关于铁路建设之条款，而《威海卫条约》则无相似规约。该条款规定，倘日后中国兴建铁路至英国控制下之九龙边界时，相关事宜需另行讨论。此一条款影响深远，概因此一条款之实施可确保香港之贸易地位。以下文字即为九广铁路之概要。

九广铁路

《展拓香港界址专条》加入铁路建设条款原因何在？1897年，通往北京之铁路干线广东—汉口段设计完成，美华合兴公司获得该线路经营特许权。有人建议在该线路临近广东终点站建造深水港。香港政府随即意识到，倘建造此一港口，却无铁路与主干线相连接，香港作为华南地区物质集散中心之地位将受到威胁。③于是英国商人与政治家纷起争夺九（龙）广（东）铁路线之经营特许权。该铁路建成之后，可与内地铁路主干线相连接，即便在广东兴建深水港计划得以实现，香港仍能保留部分贸易。在取得经营特许权后，有中英合资公司组建，虽几经拖延，最终于1905年，其从香港政府获得150万英镑贷款，

---

① 《殖民办公室列表》，1914年，第208页。
② 赫茨莱特，《中国条约》，第120页。
③ 《远东评论》，1909年11月刊，第335页。

着手兴建此一铁路。该铁路线共分两段。首段从广州至深圳（英国政府出资，交由中方管理），全长 89.5 英里，铺设于中国境内。次段深圳至九龙段长 22.5 英里，铺设于租借地之中。广州—汉口铁路线（700 英里）建成后，广九铁路不仅可加强香港与长江流域乃至北京之直接勾连，亦将促进广州之发展。

第七章

结论

第七章 结论

于前述各章节中，笔者尝试梳理了中国各租借地之状况。以下将对五个租借地做一比较，讨论租借地对中国领土主权法律效力之影响，并对这一独特而复杂之国际问题加以总结。

五个租借地之对比

就租借地本身面积而言，关东第一，面积达 1,256 平方英里；九龙第二，面积为 366 平方英里，威海卫为 285 平方英里；胶州湾为 193 平方英里；最小为广州湾，面积为 190 平方英里。从租借者来看，日本控制着面积最大之关东及胶州湾，总面积达 1,449 平方英里；英国租借之威海卫及九龙紧随其后，面积达 651 平方英里，而法国租借地广州湾，面积为 190 平方英里。

至于中立区，没有关东之中立区面积确切数据。九龙及广州湾均未设中立区。与胶州湾相连之中立区面积竟达 2,700 平方英里，威海卫中立区则为 1,505 平方英里。

就人口而言，唯一可见租借国人口大量迁入之地为关东，胶州湾亦有此趋势，然广州湾、九龙及威海卫均未见此种迹象。

就租借方式而言，德国首开武力强占胶州湾之先河，随后，列强以保障本国在华利益为借口，纷起效仿。德国人强占胶州湾之动机、倾向及最后行动均不加掩饰，路人皆知。俄罗斯与法国则臭味相投，口蜜腹剑，一再掩饰其用心，然其行径终究暴露其动机。至于英国人，其言行一向彬彬有礼，普通人殊难判断其会否言而有信。初时助中国抵制俄罗斯，后则改弦更张，加入掠夺者行列，最终竟获得两处租借地，总面积仅次于俄罗斯之租借地。对英国而言，租借威海卫情有可原，因其需要保护自身在华北贸易免受俄人侵犯。然其坚持租借九龙之意令人费解。尝有人曰："租赁九龙以卫香港。"然卫成何许人也？英国亦以俄人一直掌控关东为由，长期租借威海卫。果真如此，为何俄罗斯已失关东,英国人仍滞留威海卫?近来日本要求将关东租期延长至99年,英国是否会就威海卫租期提出类似要求?倘英人真诚维护中国权益,以此为最终目的之现实行为尚可接受。然其欧亚大陆制衡政策之最终结果不过为日本从俄国取得关东、从德国取得胶州湾而已。当然,英国人依然可以保护远东和平为由替自身辩护。

就各租借地商业贸易之重要性而言,香港乃世界上最大航运中心之一,九龙新界为香港之腹地,作用突出。在商业增长速度上,大连势头最猛。胶州湾迄今仍为贸易额最大之租借地。至于威海卫及广州湾,至今尚未显示出巨大商业价值。

从海军军事价值来看,关东之旅顺港在中国海域独占鳌头。笔者认为,九龙新界地理位置得天独厚,军事价值不输其余任何租借地;然此乃余一孔之见,并无事实可予佐证。威海卫位置虽好,但未设防。各租借地中,广州湾为公认之最无海军基地资质之所。

最后,简单比较一下列强计划以租借地为中心构建之在华势力范围,其中相关铁路线为构建势力范围之主要因素。因此,只需考察列强之铁路网建设,即可获得其构建势力范围之总体情况。在此项讨论中,可预先排除威海卫,概因英德协议规定,威海卫不可扩张势力范围。九龙新界有一条89英里铁路线连接至广州,该铁路线由英国资本家及工程师资助兴建,为香港扩张势力范围必不可少之条件,然该线路仍由中国政府控制,对英国扩张势力范围价值有限。法国人租借广州湾后,便在老街至云南府的法国铁路(248英里)沿线形成一巨大势力范围。而在胶州湾,铁路线于势力范围之影响更为明显。该铁路线全长约310英里,系由德国人出资、兴建及管理,铁路沿线自然而然纳入德国势力范围。现胶州湾虽为日军占领,然德国势力依然存在;日本作为胜利国,叫嚣要继承德国人所享有之一切权益及特权;日本人正在蚕食德国人之势力,然仍处于胶着状态。铁路线助益势力范围最显著之处当属关东。日本人在此控制着长达710英里之铁路网,

第七章　结论

守卫铁路之警事特权进一步加强了日本在关东之势力。

对中国领土主权之法律效力

虽则各租借地存在各种差异，但在租期及权益等方面，各租借地有颇多相似之处。各租借地均按租让国与租借国签订之条约租出，如有租借转让事宜，则更得依条约行事。租借地均有租期限制。租期届满前，无论何种情况中国均不得于租借地上行使管理权。中国军舰虽享有租借地港口停靠权，但需征得租借国许可。无论何种情况，租借国均有权于租借地上建造营房及防御工事。除威海卫外，列强均有依托租借地扩张势力范围之机会。以上为租借地条约订立之一般条件。而从法律层面看，各租借地对中国领土主权有何影响呢？

如系私法，租赁意味着所涉地产始终属于出租人，而承租人在协议规定之时间及条件下享有一定权益。以租赁形式租让地产时，原设保人保留与受让人同时行使所有权之权利。即使租约为永久出租，亦即受让人享有永久租赁权，罗马芝诺皇帝规定出租人仍为地产之主人。既如此，是否可以说，中国对关东、胶州湾、威海卫、九龙新界及广州湾仍然拥有主权，而日本、英国及法国仅能在租期内行使其享有之权利？对此一问题之回答，应先区分法律主权与事实主权。

就法理而言，中国不仅在租期届满后，而且在租约有效期内，均可在租借地内行使主权。因此，日本占领关东，意味着俄国租期已结束，日本如欲使此一租赁转让具备法律效力，则须获得中国之认可。此一认可权即为中国对关东租借地拥有主权之证明。胶州湾之租借转让情形类似。从法律上讲，中国仅授予租借国租借地之行政管理权，仅转让管理权而已，租赁契约不过是某种自我限制。依照国际公法，中国有权根据本国法律规定享有租借地之租赁者一应权利。

然因中国积弱，租借地之法律主权无从确保。就实际情况来看，中国之法律主权已遭严重侵害。譬如，各租借国都获得了在租借地上自由建造营房及防御工事之权利。此种情况下，倘若有国家与中国或租借国交战，租借地与交战双方关系如何处理？倘中国与他国交战，而租借国保持中立，租借地是否可视作交战区之一部分？如中国保持中立，而租借国与他国发生战争，租借地是否可视作中立区之一部分？虽则法理如此，然实际情形截然不同。日俄战争及日德战争期间租借地之情形均有悖法理。此二事件明确表明，无论是参战还是中立，租借地已然成为租借国领土之一部分；此种情况下，中国如想对租借地保持事实主权，则中国无有中立之可能；如中国欲保持其中立之可能，则事实上其对租借地之主权已受到损害。因此，应赞同劳伦斯之观点：事实上，尝试用租赁法或用益物权法中摘出之语汇将产权或领土权与土地占有权分离之说法，概属欺骗。中国真正租让者不惟领土，更有主权。

租借地之最终归宿

既如此，5处租借地之最终归宿何在？作为所有者之中国该当如何对待其名义上拥有所有权之租借地？中国最终会放弃此5处租借地之主权否，一如瑞典之放弃维斯马乎？抑或中国便如桑给巴尔，将领土永久租借与他国？抑或租期届满，中国会要求收回所有租借地耶？

必须再次呼吁诸君注意，此5处租借地乃中国之重要门户，须得中国人自己守护。一国侵犯另一国，为国家犯罪行为；然若一国任由列强围猎，则属更严重的国家犯罪行为。此一国家行为不仅危及其自身生存安全，亦将成为国际冲突之导火索。听凭外国人看守中国之门户，任由中国处于外族入侵及列强贪婪掠夺之下，会对中国及世界之和平与福祉构成威胁。为中国计，亦为全世界计，中国人有责任及使命收回租借之领土。要么收回要么亡国，中国人别无选择。

第七章 结论

如欲收回租借之领土，中国人必须做到目的一致、思想与行动统一。欲求成功之未来，且须了解过去之历史。千百年前，中国筑起了"万里长城"，此乃从中国最东部延伸到西部之巍峨城墙。至今长城依旧巍然屹立，并将永远傲然矗立，世世代代捍卫中国领土及中国人。此时此刻，中国又处生死存亡之关头，国人能否筑起"新之长城"？此一"新之长城"不再以巨石及砖块筑成，而是以四万万鲜活之肉体及灵魂，协力同心，矢志凝聚。此一"新之长城"对于收复河山必不可少；对于拱卫今后之新中国不可或缺；对于防止国际冲突、维护远东地区之国际和平亦不可少。

然而，恢复对租借地行使主权并不意味着排外。中国必须对所有国家展现宽容、公正及友好，追求国家主权及领土完整并维护世界和平。中国必须认识到自身对人类之义务。中国应以维护全人类，尤其是维护中国之利益为目标及国策为惟一正确之选。

总之，中国应保持其领土及主权完整，收回租借地。恢复中国在租借地行使主权乃吾辈一代人之责任。其他中立国应帮助实现此一目标。惟如此，远东之和平方能得到保障，"门户开放政策"方能奏效。涉利之国应将租借地还与中国，惟如此，各国方能避免与中国之冲突及相互间之冲突。中国必须明白，世界也必须清楚，中国有数百万平方英里土地可供开放，却不允许一寸土地被占领。双方均必须认识到，中国将会敞开国门，促进宗教、艺术及商业交流，但绝不会为外国强权政治敞开一扇门户。

附录

甲:参考文献

乙:汇率换算表

甲：参考文献

引言

科贝特，《国际法重要案例》，第一章，伦敦，1909年。

《外交资料汇编》（中文），上海。

科洪，《掌控太平洋》，纽约，1904年。

《美国商业关系》，华盛顿，1899—1912年。

《中国、日本、海峡殖民地、中南半岛、菲律宾等行业名录及记事》，香港，1914年。

罗伯特·道格拉斯，《欧洲与远东》，剑桥，1904年。

《远东评论》，1909年11月刊，上海，1909年。

哈特，《关注东方》，纽约，1911年。

赫茨莱特，《中国条约》，第1卷和第2卷，伦敦，1908年。

爱尔兰·阿莱恩，《中国与列强》，波士顿，1902年。

爱尔兰·阿莱恩，《远东热带》，波士顿和纽约，1905年。

《日本每周邮报》，横滨，1897—1899年。

斯科特·凯尔蒂，《政治家年刊》，伦敦，1899—1914年。

克劳塞，《远东及其历史问题》，伦敦，1903年。

克劳塞，《中国危机》，纽约，1900年。

劳伦斯，《国际法原则》，纽约，1910年。

迈克尔·麦卡锡，《未来之力量》，伦敦，1905年。

《美国领事和贸易月报》，华盛顿特区，1899—1913年。

莫里斯，《殖民化历史》，第2卷，纽约，1900年。

莫尔斯，《中国贸易与管理》，纽约，1913年。

奥本海，《国际公法》，第1卷，纽约，1905年。

佩林贾凯，《领土临时移交》，巴黎，1904年。

皮农，《为太平洋而战》，巴黎，1912年。

《美国总统咨文及外交关系》，华盛顿，1901年。

赖因施，《殖民管理》，纽约，1905年。

赖因施，《殖民政府》，纽约，1911年。

赖因施，《世界政治》，纽约，1900年。

塔迪厄，《法国与联盟》，纽约，1908年。

威尔，《东方之休战及其后果》，伦敦，1907年。

韦斯特莱克，《国际公法》，第一部分，剑桥，1910年。

伍德黑德、贝尔，《中国年鉴》，纽约，1912—1914年。

胶州湾

切拉达姆，《殖民地与德国殖民地》，巴黎，1905年。

加里斯卡尔，《德国殖民法》，吉森，1902年。

格雷西，《德国政府之拓荒与耕种工程》，华盛顿，1910年。

《英国外交部报告》，第549，2758，2790，2983，3296，3519，4508，4682，4935号。

格罗特沃德·冯·克里斯，《殖民地气候》，斯图加特，1908。

《美亚协会杂志》，纽约，1915年。

凯勒，《殖民化》，纽约，1908年。

洛伊·伊西多尔，《德国殖民财政制度》。

米尔布特，《殖民政治之使命》，墨斯，1910年。

《见地》，1914年11月刊，纽约，1914年。

赛德尔，《德国殖民地》，柏林。1909年。

托内拉，《德国于欧洲外之扩张》，巴黎，1908年。

《德国国会谈判》，柏林，1899—1913年。

关东

《德国贸易档案》，1912年版第二部分，柏林，1912年。

《英国外交部报告》，第2832, 2999, 3144, 3348, 3681, 4206, 4372, 4504, 4789, 5023号。

克劳塞，《亚洲之俄罗斯》，纽约，1899年。

劳顿·兰斯洛特，《东方帝国》第2卷，波士顿。

米勒德，《美国与远东问题》，纽约，1909年。

托克托斯，《日本年鉴》，东京，1908—1914年。

威尔，《即将到来之东亚斗争》，伦敦，1909年。

广州湾

《众议院：地方殖民预算》，巴黎，1899—1914年。

坎宁安，《法国人在东京和华南》，伦敦，1902年。

《英国外交部》报告，第2838, 2966, 3181, 3378, 3528, 3676, 3707, 3732, 4317, 4478, 4596, 4806, 4854, 4883号。

威海卫及九龙（新界）

《殖民办公室列表》，伦敦，1911—1914年。

《下议院会议报告：科马夫论文数据库》。

《英国殖民报告》，伦敦，1900—1913年。

乙：汇率换算表

中国关制白银（两，随行就市）	$ 0.70
英镑（£）	$ 4.94
法郎	$ 0.19
德国马克	$ 0.23
日元	$ 0.49
法国比索	$ 0.48
俄国卢布	$ 0.51

TAO

Leased Territories in China

Political Science

M.A.

1915

THE UNIVERSITY

OF ILLINOIS

LIBRARY

LEASED TERRITORIES IN CHINA

BY

WEN-TSING TAO

B. A. Nanking University, 1914

THESIS

Submitted in Partial Fulfillment of the Requirements for the

Degree of

MASTER OF ARTS

IN POLITICAL SCIENCE

IN

THE GRADUATE SCHOOL

OF THE

UNIVERSITY OF ILLINOIS

1915

UNIVERSITY OF ILLINOIS
THE GRADUATE SCHOOL

guue

I HEREBY RECOMMEND THAT THE THESIS PREPARED UNDER MY SUPERVISION BY   Mr. Wen-Tsing Tao

ENTITLED   Leased Territories in China

BE ACCEPTED AS FULFILLING THIS PART OF THE REQUIREMENTS FOR THE DEGREE OF   Master of Arts

Russell E.J.

In Charge of Thesis

James W.G.

Head of Department

Recommendation concurred in:*

} Committee on Final Examination*

*Required for doctor's degree but not for master's.

CHAPTER I

INTRODUCTION

CHAPTER I INTRODUCTION

By the term leased territory is meant a territory ceded by one state to another in usufruct① or in bail② for a certain period of time. Over such a territory the lessor during the period of lease, abstains from exercising any right of administration. However, on the expiration of the agreed term of lease, the lessor is entitled to receive back all rights and privileges which have been delegated.

The device of lease did not originate in China. The idea of applying to territorial transactions between states the conception drawn from Roman Law of a separation between proprietorship and beneficial enjoyment is not altogether new, though in its elaborate form we do not find it till we come to comparatively recent times. In middle ages, it took its primitive form of a pledge as when, in 1294, Edward I of England allowed Philip IV of France to hold Gascony by his garrisons, pending a settlement of various disputes between the two monarchs.③ Again, in 1803 we find a similar case in which Sweden undertook to give the town of Wismar to the Grand Duchy of Mecklenburg-Schwerin for the sum of 1,258,000 thalers, on the condition that Sweden, after the lapse of 100 years, should be entitled to take back the town on repayment of the money, with 3% interest per annum.④ Such also are the leases of different parts of his mainland dominions which the Sultan of Zanzibar granted to the British East African Company in 1888 and 1890 for 50 years, extended in 1891 to perpetuity.⑤ A similar instance is found in the

---

① Cobbet, Leading Cases on International Law, Part I, p. 110.
② Perrinjaquet, Des Cessions Temporaraires de Territoires, p. 106.
③ Lawrence, Principles of International Law, p. 175.
④ Oppenheim, International Law, vol. I, p. 221.
⑤ Westlake, International Law, Part I, p. 135.

Anglo-Congolese agreement of 12 May, 1894, whereby, the sovereign of the Congo State recognized the British sphere of influence as laid down in the Anglo-German agreement [Treaty] of 1 July, 1890 and Great Britain undertook to give that sovereign a lease of certain territories carved out of that sphere, which during his reign would include Fashoda but would afterwards be diminished in extent.[1] These examples illustrate the origin and development of the so-called "lease". But it is not until the application of the principle in China that we find it employed in such a manner as to render it conspicuous and important and worthy of special investigation.

In the year 1898, five territories with a total area of 2, 250 square miles were leased to foreign nations; that is Kiaochow[2], leased to Germany, Port Arthur and Talienwan[3], to Russia, Weihaiwei and Kowloon, to Great Britain, and Kwanchow Bay, to France. The methods of acquiring these leases were most high-handed while the conditions under which these leases were made were elaborate. It is here that we find the most highly developed form of that particular type of international transaction.

All these five territories are China's front gates; all of them are strategical point d'appui; all of them are more or less commercial centres; and all of them are the starting points of the creation of spheres of influence. Their importance to the lessor is vital and absolute and

---

[1] Westlake, International Law, Part I, p. 132, and p. 136. "A lease without any rent due from the lessee and without limit of continuance is not a true letting but an alienation." Quoted from the Revue Générale de Droit International Public.

[2] Captured by Japan in 1914.

[3] Transferred to Japan in 1905.

CHAPTER I INTRODUCTION

the possession of them by other powers is essentially detrimental and dangerous to the interest of the mother state. What then are the relations between these territories and the hinterland? How important are they as commercial centres? How important are they as naval bases? How is the process of the creation of spheres of influence going on? What is the comparative importance of each of these territories? What are the legal and actual effects of these leases on the sovereignty of China? What action should the Chinese undertake in regard to them? These are the main questions which this paper engages to discuss and answer.

CHAPTER II

KIAO CHOW

CHAPTER II KIAO CHOW

Kiao Chow, the German-leased territory in China, is situated on the coast of Shantung Province. It consists of 193 square miles, exclusive of the bay of about 200 square miles, and of a neutral zone of 2,500 square miles. The lease of this territory to Germany was sanctioned on March 6, 1898, and was governed under German administration until the 6th of November, 1914, when it fell into the hands of Japan, as a by-product of the great European War.

Viewed from its geographical position, the influence of Kiao Chow is second only to Kwantung. It is 390 miles from Shanghai, 270 miles from Weihaiwei, 334 miles from Tientsin and about 300 miles from Port Arthur.① It takes 7 hours from Kiao Chow to enter the Gulf of Peichili; 25 hours to embark at Peiho in front of Tientsin; 23 hours to reach Temulpo on the coast of Korea; 30 hours to cross the Strait of Korea and to arrive at the mediumextremity of Japan.② The importance of its geographical relation to the hinterland has led Von Richthofen, Germany's wandering geographer, to urge emphatically that Shantung is the ideal province, and Kiao Chow Bay the ideal foothold in that province for a German sphere of influence.③ Geologically speaking the same author after describing the mineral resources of the province, concluded that the power which possessed Kiao Chow would control the coal supply in northern Chinese waters.④ As a point d'appui, men have long ranked it as a second Port Arthur. Due to its rapid commercial growth, it leads people to believe that in all probability it may become

---

① China's Year Book, 1914, p. 5.
② Cheradame, La Colonisation et les Colonies Allemandes, p. 129.
③ Outlook, Nov.11,1914, P.579.
④ Kolonialzeitung, Jan. 6, 1898.

a second San Francisco.① It is due to these obvious and significant facts that Mr. Harding weightily concludes, "In the beleaguered hills that surround Tsingtao there is the key to unsuspected empire."② With respect to the psychological factor, the lease of Kiao Chow is the ear marking of the home province of the Chinese national sage, Confucius. Its occupation marks the first encroachment of foreign invasion on the mainland; it is this event that leads to the so-called the year of spoils of 1898. It is no wonder that the mention of Kiao Chow and other territories thrills the Chinese soul with indignation as the name of Alsace Lorraine stirs the soul of the French.

Germany's Colonial Ambition as a Spur to its Acquisition

During the middle period of the 19th Century, colonial possession was undervalued in Europe, especially in Germany. In his memoirs, Bismark declares that Germany, having achieved national existence and power, now has no further desire but the maintenance of peace and of the status quo. So Germany remains innocent in colonial aggression until the last two decades of the 19th Century when after unification, her economic and political situation caused her inevitably to become a seeker for colonies.③

One of the urgent causes for this change in Germany's policy is evidently found in overpopulation and emigration. This is best understood in the words of Treitochke, the fervent advocate of a

---

① Outlook, Nov. 11, 1914, p.579.
② Ibid, p. 575.
③ Reinsch, Colonial Government, p. 10.

Greater Germany. He lamented in an eloquent passage, that every year a quarter of a million Germans emigrated from the new German Empire. Treitochke desired that men and women who could not find room in Germany, should still remain German subjects under German rule when they were abroad. He said, again that in a country which had colonies to which emigrants could go, the surplus energy appeared in the Imperial balance sheet on the credit side; therefore for a growing nation, it is better to have colonies.①

Then, too, the penetration of foreign products has inspired the young patriots to set out for lands that produce such admirable goods. Germany, yearly becoming more and more industrial and commercial, is more than any other Occidental country except Great Britain dependent on foreign supplies of food and in a lesser degree on foreign supplies of raw material. This particular aspect of Germany's economic development, therefore, is also pushing her increasingly in the direction of becoming a colonial power.②

It is in these fundamental places that Germany first felt the importance of colonial acquisition due to these conditions that even Bismark was finally forced to change his efforts and attitude and in 1880 to ask the Reichstag to support private colonization. The attitude of the whole empire has changed to such an extent that the stone rejected by the builder has become the head of the corner. The common cry "too late" has been voiced, in all accents, from those of the reproachful complainer to those of the belligerent partisan and agitator. Owing to the daring

---

① The Nineteenth Century, Nov.1914, p. 959.
② Colquhoun, The Mastery of the Pacific, p.405.

and decisive measures taken by Bismark, and to the enthusiastic efforts of private individuals and companies, Germany in 1884 was successful in acquiring six territories, namely Togoland, South Africa, Kamerum, Kaiser Wilhelmland, Bismark Archipelago, and German East Africa. But unoccupied land is limited after that period, and all Germany's possessions are tropical except South Africa which is subtropical. Can Germany be satisfied with her "Imprisoned Empire" and these unavailable lands? The realization of the Welt Politik must lie in the domination over the temperate zone. China, after her war with France and Great Britain in 1860, began to disclose her weakness while the war with Japan in 1894, began to shake her foundations. Thus to the Germans China seemed to furnish one of the best opportunities for the realization of the German colonial ambition.

Balance of Power as a Cause

The balance of power in the Far East has been another strong factor that has set Germany to acquire a foothold in China. Before the lease of Kiaochow, it must be recognized that Germany was the only nation among the ambitious powers, which had decisive influence on the affairs of China. Von Bülow, in a speech given to the Reichstag, says, "It is indisputable that without a territorial point d'appui in Eastern Asia we would be simply floating in the air, from an economical, maritime and political point of view. We require an economic entrance gate to the Chinese market, as France has in Tonking, England in Hongkong, and Russia in the North... We are obliged to endeavor to obtain similar concessions to those enjoyed by other powers. Without a territorial possession, Germany's intelligence and the country's technical and commercial power would have been wasted and used merely as manure for foreign fields without fructifying our own garden. A station for the fleet was consequently an absolute necessity."① Kiao Chow, the Germans think, furnishes the most effective and most advantageous means for pursuing this end.

The Fear of Partition of China as a Motive

It is curious to notice that Germany wanted to get a foothold in China because she was afraid that China would be partitioned. In speaking to the Reichstag Chancellor Von Bülow says, "Mention has been made of a partition of China. Such a partition will not be brought about by us at any rate. All that we have to do is to provide that, come what may, we ourselves shall not go empty-handed. The traveller cannot decide when the train is to start but he can be sure not to miss it when it does start. The devil takes the hindmost."② Such a policy seems to be a far-reaching one, leading, perhaps, to partition but it becomes impossible when we carefully examine the strength of the Chinese nationality and the jealousy among the interested nations. Kiao Chow, however, to the Germans, seems to be the sure means which enables her not to miss the train. In fact, Germany has actively labored with this end in view.

---

① The Japan Weekly Mail, March 26, 1898. A similar and more detailed statement, made by von Brandt, is found in Forum, vol. 25, pp. 257–66.
② Reinsch, The World Politics, p. 164.

Steps Taken to Seize Kiao Chow Prior to Actual Occupation

The first account of Kiao Chow was made by von Richthofen, during his voyage to China in 1861. But no actual undertaking was planned until 1891 when the secret plan, as Mr. Andre Cheradame points out, was entertained by the Germans in regard to Kiao Chow.① During the Chino-Japanese War in 1894, war vessels of several nations were temporarily anchored here, so the superb position of the port was familiar to every one, especially to the Germans and the Russians. From this time on Germany's taste for Kiao Chow was intensified and her statesman worked hard toward its acquisition. The active part which Germany took with Russia and France in the retrocession of Liaotung Peninsula to China was, among other things, with a view to exacting compensation, and that compensation in the German mind was Kiao Chow.② During the visit of Lee Hung-Chang to Germany, the statesman was told that Germany was anxious to rent or buy any place upon which the two powers might agree, and that place, as understood, was Kiao Chow. The action of Germany toward Kiao Chow was further hastened by the Cassini Convention.③ In spite of doubt as to the authenticity of its contents, by Article 9 China was said to agree that Russia might lease Kiao Chow for 15 years for the use of the squadron, but in order to avoid suspicion by other powers Russia should not immediately occupy the harbor or seize

---

① R. of Rs., vol. 31, p.737. Germany's design in the Far East.
② At the time of the German seizure of Kiao Chow, the Berliner Neueste Nachrichten asserted that after all Germany did not join France and Russia in setting the differences between China and Japan in order to strengthen French and Russian interests but rather to promote her own's.
③ Cordier, Histoire, vol. 3, pp. 343–47.

CHAPTER II KIAO CHOW

the points commanding it. The Germans were impatient at the exposure of this suspected convention. So, as "The Guide to Tsingtao and its Neighborhood" tells us, on January 8, 1897, a German expert in harbor building and engineering was sent out to China by the Berlin government in response to Diedrichs' demands and as his report was again favorable, the German government made immediate overtures to the Chinese government regarding a lease of Kiaochow Bay—overtures, Which were, however, rejected but not abandoned. With the colonial aspiration among the Germans on the one hand and Richthofen's and others, exaltation of Kiao Chow on the other, the only thing for the Germans to do in realizing their dreams was to wait for an excuse which was only a matter of time.

The German Occupation of Kiao Chow

And China presented the excuse on November 1, 1897, in the death of two Roman Catholic priests, named Miel and Ziegler, living in the Chu Yi district, Yenchowfu, in the province of Shantung. On account of a long-established hatred arising from the fact that the priests in questions were disposed to help the native adherents against non-Christians, were attacked by a band of twenty ruffians, supposed to be members of the "Great Sword Society", who murdered them in cold blood. As Mr. Douglas and others point out, "This outrage differed in kind from those usually perpetrated on foreigners in that the local authorities were well-disposed towards the priests, and were in no sense promoters of the crime."[①] These extenuating circumstances were, however, entirely

---

[①] Douglas, Europe and the Far East, p.318.

ignored by the Germans who suspected the late provincial governor, Lee Pin-Hin of having instigated action. Bishop Anzer, called by Mr. Putman Weale, a German priest of the Church militant who would confound the earthly with the heavenly to serve his government, at once flashed the news to von Heyking, the German minister. Von Heyking at once got into communication with Friedrichstrasse. There was a day's interval, and then back came the order that gave von Heyking his cue. For brusque opportunism in seizing a situation it stands with the telegram of Elms. "Ask for the most exacting reparation" it ran, "and be satisfied with nothing."① The Peking government, on the other hand, promptly ordered a strict search for the culprits, and in three weeks the local authorities succeeded in arresting four of the guilty persons.

But within a few hours of the receipt of the news of the murders, the German squadron commanded by von Diedrichs, comprising the Kaiser, Prinzess, Wilhelm, and Commorant sailed from Woosung on the

---

① Harding, Outlook, Wed., Nov. 11,1914,p. 579.Mr. Reinsch in his World Politics, p. 33, says "The importance attributed to this agency (Roman Catholics), by the powers is well known by the struggle between France and Germany for the right to protect the Roman Catholic Missionaries of the Orient. France has been the traditional protector of Catholic Christians in the East. This monopoly has been the constant effort of Germany to break down by using all the influences which the Emperor could bring to bear at the Vaticans. The Emperor has asserted his right to the protectorate over certain German Communities of missionaries. And we all know how a protectorate was utilized in China, the Emperor demanding reparation for the murder of missionaries at Kiao Chow and making the outrage a pretext for gaining a permanent foothold in the Celestial Empire. His exertions to gain from the Vatican the religious protectorate in Palestine and Syria have not been successful, but he has nevertheless declared it to be his right and the policy of the German Empire to protect German missionaries wherever found." It would, however, be unjust to say that Germany is the only nation which utilizes missionaries as a means for material benefit. The fact that the flag "follows missions and trade follows the flag" has been worked out more or less by other ambitious nations. For instance, the famous case of Pere-Berthellot was utilized by France in exacting privileges in Yunnan.

CHAPTER II KIAO CHOW

11th of November and reached Kiao Chow on the 14th. Von Diedrichs sent a message to inform Chang Kao-Yuan, then General in Command of the Bay of Kiao Chow, saying that he intended landing a strong party of men and occupying the forts. The general retired on receiving a decree from Peking, and 600 German marines landed at the barracks of the fort.

The action which the Germans took was entirely contrary to the international law. It did not appear to have been preceded by any interchange of communication with the Peking government. such as the custom of nations had hitherto prescribed. The dispatch of men of war in time of peace to make a descent upon the shores of a friendly power and seize a slice of its territory, was an act that does not fall within the proper range of the doings of civilized states in the 19th Century. There was not the slightest doubt of Germany's lending herself to such performances.

After landing, on the same day, a proclamation[①] was issued to the effect that, while Germany was in friendly relations with China and had no designs on the Chinese territory[②], she intended to retain possession of the part occupied till due reparation was made for the murder of her two subjects. A few days later von Heyking, the German minister at Peking, drew up a series of demands, which were transmitted to the Chinese Foreign Office.

These demands include (1) the building of a memorial to the murdered missionaries; (2) the indemnification of the families of

---

① The Japan Weekly Mail, 1897, p. 561, p. 646.
② Does the action of lease conform to this proclamation?

the murdered men; (3) the degradation of governor Lee, in whose province the murder took place; (4) the payment of the cost of the German occupation Kiao Chow harbor; (5) the severest punishment of the murderers and local authorities; (6) the preference for German capital and engineers in the future railway and mining enterprises in the province of Shantung. The desire for the lease of Kiao Chow was still veiled.①

While consenting to these demands, the Chinese Foreign Office requested the evacuation of Kiao Chow. In reply to this, Germany gave an unqualified refusal, and added that further guarantees were required for the protection in the future of the life of German subjects all over China. Taking this as a justification, Germany now openly expressed a wish to lease Kiao Chow and territory inland, a demand which was contradictory to her former declaration.

At the same time, with great ostentation, Prince Henry of Prussia, the brother of the Kaiser was dispatched at the head of an expedition by the Kaiser to China. The Kaiser at a banquet given at Kiel Castle on December 15, 1897, previous to the sailing of the German squadron for China, in toasting Prince Henry, said, "The expedition which you undertake is the logical consequence of what our sainted grandfather and his great chancellor have politically organized and what our illustrious father won by hie sword on the battlefield. They were naught but the first realization of the Trans-Oceanic ambition of the newly united and newly arisen German Empire. German commerce flourishes and develops; and it can only develop in prosperity and safety when it feels safe under the

---

① Presidential Message and Foreign Relations of the United States, 1898, p. 188.

CHAPTER II KIAO CHOW

Imperial power...Imperial power is sea power; sea power and Imperial power are mutually dependent on each other, so much so that one can not exist without the other. May our citizens abroad rest absolutely assured that the protection of the empire will everywhere be given. Should anyone infringe our just right or injure us, then up at him with your Mailed Fist (Fahre dem mit gepanzerter Faust) , and if it be God's Will, weave for your youthful brow a wreath of laurel which no one in all the German Empire will grudge you." Prince Henry in an extraordinary response said, "My only aim is to preach abroad the gospel of your sacred Majesty (Das Evangelism Eurer Majestat geheiligter Person in Auslande zu kunden) . to preach to everyone who will hear it, and also to those who will not hear it. This gospel I will have inscribed on my banner and I will inscribe it whithersoever I go."[①]

Although these Kiel speeches were ridiculed as being more suitable to heroes of melodrama, either as verging on blasphemy or as altogether incomprehensible, yet they served quite well to indicate the German attitude toward the Far East. They were, though empty, yet loud enough to hasten the lease of Kiao Chow, which took place on the 5th of January 1898, two months before the signing of the treaty[②], and over four months before the Prince's formal audience with Emperor Kuan Tsu.

---

① The two speeches are fully given in The Japan Weekly Mail, 1898, pp. 85–8.
② The treaty was signed at Peking by Lee Hung-Chang, Weng-Tung Ho and von Heyking on the 6th of March, 1898, see Hertslet's China Treaties, vol. 1, p. 350.

Government under German Rule

The administration after the lease was entrusted to the navy department, and a naval officer was placed at its head with the title of governor. The council is composed of all the heads of the administrative departments under the personal supervision of the governor and four members chosen from the civil population and appointed for two years; the first was named by the governor, with the consent of the council, the second was chosen from among the members of the non-Chinese firms, the third from the list of taxpayers paying at least $50 Ground Tax, without distinction of nationality, and the fourth from the committee of the Chamber of Commerce. There were judicial officers for European residents, with an appeal to the German Consular Court at Shanghai; Chinese residents were subject to this jurisdiction only in special cases.

Germany's Policy in Kiao Chow after Occupation

After having surveyed the manner of Germany's acquisition of Kiao Chow, it is not hard to determine her policy of administration and its keynote may be immediately noticed from von Diedrichs' proclamation in Chinese: "Be it known to all concerned that I have come in obedience to the commands of my sovereign, his Majesty the German Emperor, who has instructed me to land at Kiao Chow Bay at the head of my forces, and seizes the said Bay and all the islands and dependencies thereof. Avoid resisting whatever the German authorities shall decide to do hereafter. You should calculate the exigencies of the case, and you will see that you are too weak to resist. Not only will you find it to

CHAPTER II KIAO CHOW

be of no advantage to you but you will find that you will have invited destruction upon yourselves."①

Like strong personalities, Germany as well as other nations is filled with a desire to impress the mark of her genius upon the world. This is one of the things which she has been intending to do in China. In their heart of hearts there can be no truer gratification than that of hearing their languages spoken in a strange land, than that of having their customs and institutions acknowledged as superior by other races, and above all than having their grandeur and might worshipped and praised by foreign lands ignoring the first two, the last is best expressed in the words of von Bülow: "The best pledge for the future is, in our view, the presence of German ships of war and of a German garrison in Kiao Chow Bay. The might of the German Empire is thus constantly and visibly exhibited to the local authorities as well as its population."②

And again when emphasizing the seizure of Kiao Chow he said: "We have secured in Kiao Chow a strategical and political position which assures us a decisive influence on the Far East. From this strong position, we can look with complacency on the development of affairs. German diplomacy will pursue its path in the East as elsewhere—calmly, firmly and peacefully."

---

① The Times, Jan. 6, 1898.
② Ibid, Jan. 25, 1898. These reveal the fact that in all Germany's administration in Kiao Chow, the rights and feelings of the Chinese residents were disregarded. What was adopted, was adopted in the interest of the Germans. This territory before the European War broke out might be said to be a territory of the Germans, by the Germans, and for the Germans. As to the natives, in all affairs, they had no representation though they paid an ever-increasing tax. There is some reason therefore why the Germans are called "red devils" in Kiao Chow. But it must be noticed that the German administration in Kiao Chow had been much milder and more reasonable if we compare it with the Russian and the Japanese administration in Kwantung.

In short, applying artificial force and to providing arbitrary conditions regardless of Chinese interests in the creation of a permanent commercial centre and the establishment of a permanent naval base in Kiao Chow have been Germany's primary policy, and her ultimate policy is to create a sphere of influence and interest with Kiao Chow as a starting point. In order to understand these policies better, it is necessary to have a digest of the treaty and conventions between China and Germany which defines the scope of action, and a bird's eye view of the works which the Germans have undertaken and which constitute the actual expression of these policies.

A Digest of Treaty and Conventions

In the first place, China is entitled to receive rent from the German government for the lease of Kiao Chow. This is, however, considered by the Germans as only a matter of formality. In speaking to the Reichstag von Bülow has referred to this matter. "The rent," he says, "to be paid, will in no case be a large one, since it is not meant as something paid for the leased land, but is simply a formality of the nature of what jurists call a recognition payment, implying an acknowledgment of the continuance of theoretical possession on the part of the Emperor of China."[①]

By the convention of 1906[②], the Chinese Imperial Maritime Customs collects duties at the leased port and the customs director is to be appointed jointly by the German minister at Peking and the

---

① A full copy of the speech is given in The Japan Weekly Mail, March 26, 1898, p. 326.
② A full treatment is given under the heading of "Kiao Chow as a Port."

CHAPTER II KIAO CHOW

Commissioner of the Chinese Imperial Customs.

In short, within the limit① of the leased 193 square miles, the Chinese government abstains from exercising rights of sovereignty during the term of the lease except the right of receiving a trifling rent and a partial power of collecting customs duties. With these exceptions Germany can do anything as she pleases.

In regard to the 50 kilometer neutral zone surrounding the Kiao Chow Bay at high water, the Chinese reserved to themselves all rights of administration except in two cases: first, China has the right to station troops and to take other military measures within the zone, in doing this, she must be in agreement with the Germany government while the free passage of the German troops within this zone is permitted at all times; Second, without the previous consent of the German government China abstains from taking any measures or issuing any ordinances. With respect to the mining and railway concessions, the four articles leave China in a helpless position. It is true that the Chinese merchants may take shares in the formation of the Deutsche-Chinesische Gesellschaft, which is established for the construction of the two conceded railway lines.② It is still true that the work of excavating coal within 10 miles along the railways may be undertaken by Chinese and German merchants combining their capitals. But the concluding section explicitly states that if within the province of Shantung any matters are undertaken, for which foreign capital or assistance is invited, China agrees that the German merchants concerned shall first be asked whether they wish to undertake

---

① Hertslet, China Treaties, p. 352.
② Detail treatment is given under railways in connection with Kiao Chow.

the works and provide the materials. That is to say, only when foreign capital is unnecessary and neither the German government nor German capitalists will look at a scheme, is China graciously permitted to do as she pleases in her own territory. This, together with the conceded railways and mines, in reality, constitutes the prophecy of a sphere of influence in the hinterland.

Finally, the provision of the return to China of Kiao Chow before the expiration of lease, puts China in a most difficult and indefinite position. The article runs "Should Germany (not China), at some future time express the wish to return Kiao Chow Bay to China before the expiration of the lease, China engages to refund to Germany the expenditure she has incurred at Kiao Chow and to cede to Germany a more suitable place." It means that China has to refund the incurred expenditure and China has to cede a more suitable place, should Germany return Kiao Chow under such conditions. The insertion of this article has two obvious aims: (1) After a sphere of influence has been thoroughly established in the hinterland, if Kiao Chow were returned to China, it would still fall under the German influence and China would be helpless to control this separated bit of territory. But Germany would be able to gain a more suitable place and would be able to utilize the returned expenditure to build a new commercial and political centre and would be able to start another sphere of influence. (2) We must remember that Germany leases Kiao Chow as a protection of German interests in China but what protection has she for the safety of Kiao Chow itself? It is unquestioned that Germany has tried her best to build strong forts on it. But can Germany do anything to protect this isolated territory in case of unexpected conflict between the Imprisoned Empire and other powers especially England and Japan? The cautious Teuton thus made every arrangement to wriggle out, should he be forced by events to do so. With respect to the first project, conditions perhaps will never permit its realization. It is in the second aim that we find the far-reaching policy of the Germans, but Japan has risen up to take measures before Germany expressed any intention of turning it over to China.

A General Survey of Germany's Efforts in the Building up of Kiao Chow

Kiao Chow, before the German lease, was only a small hamlet consisting of a population of about 500. Its development is undoubtedly an exceedingly difficult and most expensive task. It is here, as well as in Kamerum, Togoland and other places, that we see the Germany's liberal attitude, the strenuous efforts, and her strong courage in a distant territory.

From 1899 up to the Japanese seizure, a period of fifteen years, the annual average Imperial subvention for Kiao Chow was about 10,000,000 marks, against an annual average expenditure of 13,000,000 marks. The most expensive fiscal year under the German administration was found in 1905–06 [1904–05], when the total expenditure was 15,296,000 marks out of which sum, 14,000,000 marks constituted a subvention from the Imperial Government. During the entire fifteen years, the Imperial Government has paid 156,000,000 marks in subventions, against a total expenditure of 185,000,000 marks. The enormous sum which has been spent on the building of Kiao Chow is seen in the following table.

Date	Expenditure (Marks)	Imperial Subvention (Marks)
1899–1900	8,500,000	8,500,000
1900–1901	9,780,000	9,780,000
1901–1902	12,528,000	
1902–1903	12,876,000	12,168,000
1903–1904	13,088,000	12,421,000
1904–1905	15,296,000	12,583,000
1905–1906	13,278,000	14,000,000
1906–1907		11,735,000
1907–1908		
1908–1909	12,327,000	10,601,600
1909–1910	12,352,597	
1910–1911	12,722,000	
1911–1912	13,540,000	7,704,000
1912–1913	16,640,000	8,293,000
1913–1914	16,783,625	9,560,000

From the above table we see that except the period between (1902—07) when harbors and other great works were in the process of construction, the Imperial Subvention remains stationary between the minimum of 7,000,000 and the maximum of 11,000,000, while revenues and expenditure increase proportionately. The enormous increase in expenditure accounts for the prosperity off the territory and the enormous increase in revenue gives promise of a self-supporting colony. It is quite probable that a yearly surplus of revenue over expenditure may be attained as is the case in Hongkong. It might be a good thing if the Kaiser's declaration "Kiao Chow musz uns bleiben" might be realised for then Germany may reap the harvest for which she has toilsomely worked. But the chance seems in all respect to be favorable to fortune-hunting Japan.

If we are asked in what way have the expenditures been spent and from what source have the revenues been drawn, the best answer we have at our disposal is found in the Budget of 1905-06, a most active year, which is given as follows:

Budget for Kiao Chow
(April 1, 1905 –March 31, 1906)

I. Revenue
(in pound sterling)

Sales of land	2,447
Direct taxes	4,406
Other receipts	24,279
Imperial subsidy	717,607
Total	748,739

II. Expenditure
(in pound sterling)

Recurring expenditure

Civil administration	53,928
Naval administration	74,257
Chinese regiment	1,346
Rations	30,894
Clothing	10,655

Artillery and fortification 15,595

Maintenance of public buildings 17,685

Horses harness, carts 8,865

Public worship and education 3,493

Hospitals and sanitary service 17,698

Treasury 5,586

Miscellaneous... 53,556

Pension fund 441

Total-recurring expenditure 293,999

Non-recurring expenditure

Harbor works 170,004

Buildings and land purchase 96,138

Industrial dwelling 4,895

Forestry and regulation of streams 3,916

Armaments 122,375

Bouys and Surveys.. 1,958

5th installment floating docks 53,845

For unforeseen expenses 1,609

Total non-recurring expenditure 453,640

Grand total 748,739

From the above table, we learn that out of a total expenditure of £748,739, £223,849 were used in the construction of harbor, and floating docks, £222,438 were used in military and naval works and only £53,928 for civil administration. The harbors and docks are directly related to naval administration so out of the total expenditure,

60% were spent for military and naval purposes. The fortifications, harbor and docks further have to be continued for many years before reaching completion.

Besides these expenditures, the Schangtung Eisenbahn Gesellschaft was formed in June 1899, with a capital of 54,000,000 marks (£ 2,700,000), to construct the railways. Two famous mining companies, the Schangtung Bergbaugesellechaft and the Deutsche Gesellechaft fur Bergbau and Industrie im Auelande have been successively established for exploitation. The former was organized by some of the most powerful German bankers and with a capital of 12,000,000 marks (£ 600,000), while the latter was aKolonial Gesellschaft, a species of chartered company, with powers conferred on it by the Bundesrath.

Thus from the year 1898 when the territory was leased up to the Japanese occupation, it is estimated that $123,575,000 a sum which equals half of the Russian investment in Manchuria ($ 257,500,000) up to 1904, has been spent by the German government and the railway and mining companies acting under the government supervision in the development of Kiao Chow.

The Deutsche Asiatische Bank with a capital of 5,000, 000 taels, and some minor corporations such as the Commercial Association of Shantung with a capital of 240,000 marks and the Kiao Chow Association with a capital of 204,000 marks have also taken active part in the development of Kiao Chow.

Thus to the Germans, colony acquisition has proved itself an expensive luxury. They seem to regard it worth the cost. The enormous increase in revenue has already given assurance to their expectation. And as Mr. Keller says, "By this lavishness, the Germans thought to raise the importance of the empire in the eyes of the world.

In addition to the pouring in of capital which overwhelms Kiao Chow, we find there an army of penetration of officials, soldiers, engineers, and fortune hunters who call themselves patriots and who sow the seed which, they hope, will steadily "expand into a beautiful Imperial tree" on which they hope to hang "an eastern policy of a most astonishing character."

So much for the general survey of Germany's effort in developing Kiao Chow; let us now pass to a view of some of the most important works in a somewhat detailed manner.

Tsingtao as a port

Tsingtao is the name of the port, and Kiao Chaw, that of the whole territory. On September 2, 1895, it was declared a free port, and the Chinese Imperial Custom House collected duties at the railway station. But in 1906 a new convention came into force whereby Tsingtao ceased to be a free port, and the Chinese Imperial Maritime Customs now collects duties here as at all the other treaty ports of China. But the convention among other things stipulates that 20 % of the money so collected at Tsingtao shall be paid to the German Government. According to the statistics of the year 1912, the customs revenue amounts to 1,670,029 taels out of which 334,006 taels are turned over to Germany. Is it not interesting to observe that China has leased this territory for a trifling rent which von Bülow called simply a "recognition payment"and yet now the owner must pay 334,006 taels to the tenant for the establishment of a customs house on it? This change,which,in Mr

CHAPTER II KIAO CHOW

Rockhill's words, is on each side of the nature of a special concession for special consideration, will, however, facilitate work for both merchant and customs officers, as well as increase revenue, in addition to placing the Kiao Chow customs house function in Tsingtao on an improved footing.[①] This together with the new customs arrangement in 1909 has contributed some to the promotion of trade at Kiao Chow. The growth of trade at Kiao Chow from 1900 to 1912 is seen in the following table:[②]

Date	Import (hk. tls.)	Export (hk. tls.)
1900	158,598	32,282
1901	2,527,609	18,370
1902	3,678,690	105,272
1903	5,134,229	234,216
1904	3,437,897	845,302
1905	4,372,937	2,430,350
1906	7,019,263	3,540,123
1907	7,297,944	887,226
1908	8,266,562	2,707,707
1909	10,655,398	3,359,386
1910	25,409,209	17,171,415
1911	26,287,988	19,853,669
1912	29,742,731	24,999,360

From 1900 to 1912 the value of trade at Kiao Chow multiplied 280 times while the customs revenue multiplied as many as 300 times. Within the last five years, it has risen from the twenty-second port in the amount of revenue that its customs receipts turn into the Chinese government, to

---

① U. S. Consular and Trade Reports, 1906, p. 179.
② Statesman's Year Book, 1902–1914.

the sixth port, being exceeded in its business, as indicated in this unique record, only by Shanghai, Tientsin, Hankow, Canton and Swatow. Dairen is the seventh, being 260,000 tls, below Kiao Chow. Dairen of course has moved more rapidly than has Kiao Chow. In 1907 Dairen's revenue amounted to 140,738 taels. but increased to 1,407,926 taels. in 1912, while the revenue of Kiao Chow increased from 934,623 taels. in 1907 to 1,670, 029 tls in 1912. The rate of increase of the revenue of Kiao Chow during this period is only one sixth as rapid as that of Dairen. Although Dairen has in five years almost matched Kiao Chow in trade, it is still safe to say that except Dairen no other port in China has grown as Kiao Chow has grown, and no other port save. Dairen and Shanghai can stand the pace Kiao Chow has set.

However, it should not be overlooked that the commerce of this port is not yet entirely free from the artificial conditions under which it was created. The prosperity of its trade still depends more or less on the disbursements of the government. The frequent report of the Japanese inability to restore its commerce, if substantiated, will prove the truth of this.

Kiao Chow Ray as a Naval Base

The bay itself has been described as the natural entrance and exit for Shantung and the maritime key of the province. This is a thing which Germany has hunted for years in Chinese waters. This is a thing which is essential to the realization of the Kaiser's ambition, "Imperial power means sea power." So the construction of a naval base at Kiao Chow Bay deserves immediate consideration.

As soon as the Germans took over control, the present vast scheme of fortifications, already decided upon, was inaugurated by an army of engineers and skilled workmen specially sent from home. They constructed a ring of 12 modern forts, stretching from the high, rocky peninsula of Laoshan on the north, along the thickly wooded ridges back of Tsingtao, 6 miles from the harbor mouth, and out again along the southern peninsula of Lingshan. They spent $ 7,000,000 in dredging the harbor and the bay; they constructed a floating dock capable of lifting 16,000 tons; they sunk granite piers about 2,000 meters long, and built a modern graving dock capable of accommodating the largest merchant ships and men-of-war afloat. In ten years $ 30,000,000 was spent on harbor works alone. Shipbuilding is carried on at the naval base, both for merchantile trade and naval purposes. Indeed, it would be possible, given the raw materials, to build and equip anything up to second-class cruisers. The barracks, built in 1908, were capable of housing 5,000 men; and the 3,000 first sent out have been steadily increased till before the war the regular forces defending the territory, excluding 2,500 volunteers from the settlement itself, numbered over 6,000 including a squadron of cavalry, a company of field artillery, two machine gun companies, five companies of naval artillery, one aeroplane corps of four units, and a company of native reserves. [1] The Kiao Chow service was popular in Deutschland, and young men from the best families entered it with the double purpose of serving their country and indulging their curiosity in regard to the Far East.

The military necessity of the leased territory has begun only in the

---

[1] Outlook, Nov. 11, 1914, p. 582.

present decade to make way for the industrial campaign for which it has always been the far-reaching ground-breaker. Invariably up to the year before last （1913）, out of an average budget of 13,000,000 marks, something like 10,000,000 marks have been contributed by the Imperial Treasury for these extraordinary expenditures. It is said that the Prussian officers have spent ten dollars on military works to every one dollar on the civilian population.

The two coal fields at Weihsien and Poshan which are near the port are averaging today an annual production of just a half million tons and renders Kiao Chow a good coaling station for a fleet and other ships.

Furthermore, the decision of the German exploiting company, the Schangtung Eisenbahn Gesellschaft, to spend $ 12,000,000 on the erection of a vast steel and iron plant at Tsingtao makes men feel that great plans are working out in their development and approaching nearer and nearer to their practical realization. At the same meeting, on 5 January 1914, it was decided to include an arsenal in the new works. This plan, if completed, would have been able to furnish anything essential to the formation of Kiao Chow into the strongest naval and military foothold in the Far East.

Railways in Connection with Kiao Chow

Frederick List, the German economist, has long since unfolded the principle that communication, politics, and commerce must go hand in hand. Kiao Chow furnishes its concrete manifestation. It was Germany's ambition to create out of Kiao Chow a second San Francisco, and to

CHAPTER II KIAO CHOW

build in Shantung a sphere of influence which will control the vast hinterland. How did she plan for it? Nothing short of a vast scheme of railways could accomplish that end. Imperial power means not only naval power, but also means railway power. It is exceedingly interesting that in Kiao Chow we find that the Imperial power has tried to manifest itself through both channels.

In connection with the lease of Kiao Chow, China agrees to permit Germany to construct two railways in the province of Shantung: one from Kiao Chow, past Weihsian, Chingchow, Poshan, Tsuchuan,and Tsonping to Tsinan and the Shantung frontier; the other from Kiao Chow to Ichow and thence past Laiwuhsien to Tsinan. The railway from Tsinan to the frontier of Shantung is not to be constructed until the main line is completed and its route is still left to be determined.[1] The proposed line between Ichow and Tsinan was abandoned in favor of the Chinese Imperial Tientsin-Pukow Railway which is financed by the Anglo-German Syndicate and managed by the Chinese government.[2] The Kiao Cow—Ichow line was surveyed but further work was abandoned.[3] So the only railway conceded to Germany requiring consideration is the line between Kiao Chow via Weihsien and Poshan to Tsinan.

This railway was conducted by the Schangtung Eisenbahn Gesellschaft which was organized in Berlin with a capital of 54,000,000 marks. The main line from Tsingtao—Tsinan, a distance of 256 miles was opened to traffic in June, 1904. The two branches, Changtien—Poshan and Tsaochuan—Taichuan respectively, were opened to traffic in

---

[1] Hertslet, China Treaties, vol. l, p. 353.
[2] The Far Eastern Review, Nov. 1909, p. 286.
[3] Ibid.

1910. Taking them all together it makes a total trackage of 310 miles.[①]

The opening of the main line dates the commercial prosperity of the settlement. "This is not to be wondered at being put in possession of a first-class harbor and a railway connecting with the very heart of the most densely populous country in the world, hitherto without means of communication, the prosperity of Kiao Chow worked its own way."[②] The yearly value of trade at Kiao Chow has already been discussed in a former section, let us now see what proportion of the trade this railway carries since its inauguration:

Date	Annual passengers (Heads)	Annual freight (Tons)	Annual net profit (Marks)
1904	558,868	179,270	
1905	803,527	310,482	2,063,572
1906	846,000	381,000	2,642,000
1911	909,065	717,189	4,731,238
1912	1,230,043	852,001	7,050,000

According to these figures, during the last eight years, passenger traffic has more than doubled, freight traffic has increased more than 4 times while the net profit has increased 3.5 times. The proportional increase in traffic of the past shows still a greater volume of transactions is to come in the future. The net profit of 1912 was high enough to compensate for the Imperial subvention, being 7,000,000 marks against 7,704,000 marks.

One of the direct effects of this railway is the retarding of the trade

---

① China's Year Book, 1914, p. 213.
② Journal of the American Asiatic Association, January 1915, p.367.

of Chefoo, the Chinese treaty port, which is shown in the following table:①

Date	Import (hk.tls.)	Export (hk.tls.)
1905	9,607,561	4,677,509
1906	7,906,839	4,806,654
1907	6,620,215	3,299,002
1908	6,182,640	3,524,592
1909	5,999,755	4,037,687
1910	15,464,159	14,731,624
1911	16,654,026	13,916,518
1912	15,872,719	12,863,731

From the above table we notice that from the opening of the railway, the imports of Chefoo decreased, from 9,607,561 hk. tls. to 5,999,755 hk.tls. while exports decreased from 4,677,509 hk.tls. to 4,037,687 hk.tls. There was a sudden increase of trade value in Chefoo from 1910② due to the opening of the northern section of the Tientsin-Pukow Railway, yet after the sudden increase its trade remains practically stationary while during the same time the trade of Kiao Chow has increased 20%.③ A more striking illustration of the decline of Chefoo and the rise of Kiao Chow will be noticed in the amount of revenue collected at each of the ports:④

---

① Statesman's Year Book, 1907–1914.
② China's Year Book, 1914, p. 223.
③ Ibid.
④ Ibid, p.139 and p. 122. However, we must admit that according to recent reports of the customs house, the trade of Chefoo during 1912 and 1913 has shown some increase and has kept up well.

Date	Customs revenue at Chefoo (hk.tls.)	Customs revenue at Kiao Chow (hk.tls.)
1905	871,607	545,150
1906	818,322	863,430
1907	633,243	934,623
1908	644,914	926,716
1909	748,338	1,120,243
1910	651,265	1,238,394
1911	595,914	1,251,001
1912	704,735	1,670,029

From the year 1905 up to 1912, while Kiao Chow as a port rises from the 16th, place to the 6th place, Chefoo drops from the 10th to the 14th among the 47 ports according to the total amount of customs revenue collected at each port.

Not only does the revenue of maritime customs show the decline of Chefoo, but the revenue of the native customs, which exists side by side with the former, shows the conclusion even more clearly. In 1909 it was estimated at 97,609 hk.tls., it decreased to 76,262 hk.tls. in 1910, a little rise in 1911, but in 1912 it suddenly decreased to 68,823 hk.tls.

The case is also remarkably illustrated in the trade of straw braid; of the total export of this product of home industry from the two Shantung ports in 1903, Chefoo contributed 70% and Kiao Chow, 30%. The change took place so remarkably that Kiao Chow has entirely displaced Chefoo in this export. This is clearly shown in the following table:[1]

---

[1] House of Commons Sessional Paper, 1912—13, vol. 95, p.79, p.183.

CHAPTER II KIAO CHOW

Date	Kiao Chow (cwts)	Chefoo (cwts)
1908	99,701	930
1909	125,315	388
1910	119,068	225
1911	104,764	5

The railway has also enabled Tsingtao to capture practically the whole of the raw silk and ground nut trade from Chefoo.

Another important direct effect of this railway concession is to be found in the scheme of the Chinese Tientsin-Pukow Railway. The original concession for the railway from Tientsin to Chinkiang was granted in 1897 to Dr. Yung Wing, with permission to enlist the aid of foreign capital. Dr. Yung Wing entered into negotiations with American and British capitalists for a loan which was estimated as $ 27,000,000 gold. The Germans aimed at the abolition of Dr. Yung's noble plan by seeking to apply to it the special privileges which were officially granted in 1898, many months later than the sanction of Dr. Yung's plan. Germany's demand was evidently a violation of the agreement which provided for German participation in foreign loans only after its signing. But Germany finally blocked further hope for Dr. Yung and the American capitalists.[①] An agreement was formally signed and sealed in 1898, which provided that the construction and control of the railway should be held in the hands of the Chinese government and that the Anglo-German Syndicate should furnish a loan of £ 5,000,000, some materials and engineers. The British and German chief engineers were, however, subordinated to the control of the Chinese managing director.

---

① The Far Eastern Review, 1909, November No. p.309.

Having surveyed some of the effects of the Tsingtao-Tsinan Railway concession, let us now see what an important position Tsingtao occupies on account of the very important matter of railway connections.

In the first place, the Tsinan- Tientsin Railway connects Tsing-tao With Tientsin, Peking, Mukden, Zhangjiakou, Saint Petersburg, Berlin, and the rest of Europe through the northern section of the Tientsin Pukow Railway（390½ miles）, Peking-Mukden Railway（527 miles）, Peking-Kalgan Railway（124 miles）, The Chinese Eastern Railway（1081 m.） and the trans-Siberian Railway. The projected extension （600 miles） of the Peking-Zhangjiakou Railway through Suiyuanhen, Tatungfu, and Urga will render a more immediate connection between Tsingtao and the trans-Siberian Railway at Hailar. The southern section of the Tientsin-Pukow Railway（236½ miles）,furnishes a connection between Tsingtao and Nanking, the ancient capital of China, and thereby the Shanghai-Nanking Railway（193 miles） and the Kiangsu-Chekiang Railway （241 miles） connect Tsingtao with Shanghai, Hangchow and Ningpo. By way of the Yangtze River via the projected line between Nanchang and Chaochow; and the Chaochow-Swatow line, one can reach the coast of Fukien at Swatow. Towards the end of 1913, it was announced that the German government had concluded an agreement with China for the construction of other lines. First, the Kaomi-Han-chwang line will draw to Tsingtao not only more iron and coal but also beans and wheat. Second, a line has been projected connecting the Tientsin-Pukow Railway and the Peking-Hankow Railway （755 miles）, between Tsinan and Shunteh.① This will enable Tsingtao to come into direct communication with Hankow, the so-called the

---

① China's Year Book, 1914, p. 210.

CHAPTER II KIAO CHOW   143

Chicago of China; and through the projected Hankow-Canton Railway, Tsingtao will be able to effect indirect communication with Canton. A more important scheme is seen in the Yenchow-Kaifen Railway. Yenchow is already in connection with Tsingtao through the Tientsin-Pukow Railway. It was Germany's secret plan to connect Yenchow with Kaifen so that Tsingtao may in the future have direct communication on one hand with Honan, Tongkuan, Sianfu, Lanchow, and Ili through the projected North-Western Grand Trunk System which will, as Mr. Harding says, "one day pierce the heart of the Asiatic continent from the trans-Caspian outposts of Russia three thousand miles across the vast unknown deserts of Chinese Turkestan and will sweep thence through the centre of China to the sea; on the other hand, the connection with Chunking, Chengtu, and French Indo-China thru the projected Sian-Chunching, Yunnan-French Indo-China line of which 1,400 miles connection southward to Chungking have already been guaranteed and signed. The Yenchow-Kaifen line has already been surveyed by the Germans in 1910, and constitutes a branch of the German section of the Tientsin-Pukow Railway. For the moment the line ends at Tsiningchow but the course planned indicates that it will be continued to Kaifen. Tsingtao then having this line in connection with the splendid harbor which she has at her disposal will naturally serve as the outlet of these vast systems."

From the above survey, it is thus safe to conclude that northward, southward, and westward Tsingtao will be all powerful as soon as these railway systems have been completed. As in Manchuria, everything here has been planned on the moat extensive scale, and everywhere there is evidence that a notable future is being thought of.[①]

Other Works Undertaken by Germany

It has been pointed out in the former paragraphs that Germany's ambition is not only to create at Kiao Chow a commercial centre and a naval base but also to create a sphere of influence in the hinterland. While under railways and military undertakings Germany's aims have been touched upon, some other miscellaneous attempts will here be discussed.

(a) Coal Mining. The railway concession carries with it the right of mining. The treaty stipulates that Germany can mine coal within the 30-kilometer zone. But, as Mr. Weale points out, the fields are far beyond the legal limit. The annual production was constantly increasing until 1912, it reached over a half million tons or one two thousand three hundred and thirtieth of the world's production. Its annual production is presented here:

Date	Fantze mine (tons)	Hungshan mine (tons)	Total (tons)
1907	145,000	34,200	179,200
1908	222,450	56,600	279,050
1909	272,000	160,000	432,000
1910	230,064	252,816	482,880
1911	184,233	302,300	486,533
1912			573,676

(b) Afforestation. In Kiao Chow as in other German colonies,

---

① The treatment of this section is based on the data furnished in China's Year Book, 1914, pp. 208–244.

scientific investigations of the most valuable kind have been made in coincidence with the advance of expeditions and of the administrative station, and this is found in the work of afforestation. One hundred and forty-four acres of land have been put under cultivation; a million of trees and plants have been sold to natives annually. This work is very productive in Kiao Chow. An annual revenue of about 100,000 marks has been drawn from this source.[1]

(c) Post Office. The Deutsche Reichspost has made its way in inland. On every German train a section of a carriage is given up to the German postal authorities. It has maintained a rate-cutting competition against the Chinese post office.

(d) Attempts to secure advisorship. It has also been stated by Mr. Weale that the Germans have been trying very hard to obtain the appointment of a German foreign advisor to the governor of Shantung.

(e) Missionary Works. "As in Occidental Africa", Mr. Cheradame remarks, "the German missionaries prepare for political penetration."[2] He even goes so far as to include missions under administrative organization. In fact, Bishop Anzer, the head of the Catholic Mission in Shantung has declared that the occupation of Kiao Chow is a matter of life and death to German missionaries.[3] In exciting public sentiment to aspire for the union of missions and colonial policy, the German professor, Mr. Mirbt has openly declared, "Such Mission and Kolonial Politik gehoren zusammen undwir haben Grund zu der Hoffnung, dasz

---

[1] House of Commons Sessional Paper, 1912–13, vol.75–183.
[2] Cheradame, La Colonisation et le colonies Allemande, p.127.
[3] See von Bülow's Speech, The Japan Weekly Mail, March, 1898.

aus diesen Bund gutes fur unsere Kolonien erwachsen vird."①

The present German missionary force in Kiao Chow consists of fifteen ordinary and three extraordinary missionaries. Although the writer believes there must be some who are sincere in their spiritual purpose yet the fact that they receive financial assistance from the government tends to oblige them to work for their Vaterland as well as for the Kingdom of God.②

(f) Education. The process of Germanizing this leased territory will not be completed without a predominance of German culture. This is done in the establishment of schools. "Tsingtao", one writer remarks, "has more schools and gymnasiums than any other town of the same size."③ Segregation between the Chinese and Europeans is rigorously insisted on. Nine schools are directly supported by the German government. Mr. Mirbt has plainly told us, "die Eroberung unserer Kolonien durch die Schulen" because, he thinks, "die Leute verlangen allenthalben nach efner bessern Bildung und namentlich nach einer Kenntis des Deutschen."④ However, It must be given credit that some young men are indebted to these schools for their inspiration toward scientific research.

(g) Land Questions. The Germanization of Kiao Chow will not be completed without the entire deprivation of land ownership of the Chinese residents. If the Chinese wished to sell any land, they could only sell to the German government, who sold it on to European settlers,— almost entirely Germans.⑤ The buyer of land must pay a tax of 33% of

---

① Mirbt, Mission und Kolonial Politik, p. 4, p.71.
② The German Colonial System, p. 3.
③ Journal of the American Asiatic Association, January 1915, p.365.
④ Mirbt, Mission und Kolonial Politik, p.158.
⑤ Colquhoun, The Mastery of the Pacific, p. 409.

the cost, and if the plot of land is not sold for 25 years, the owner of the land has to give notice of any intended sale and the government has the first option to buy at the owner's figure. Every land owner has to pay each year a tax of 6% of the capital value. If the land was not being built upon at a certain date stipulated in the plan of building, the owner forfeited the right of property and the government took it up, paying only half the assessed value. This was, however, changed by the order of December 31, 1903, which provides a progressive land value tax instead of forfeiting the right of property.[1] At any rate, the German government has been trying to take the entire control of land property in Kiao Chow out of the hand of the Chinese. Evidently Germany, under the disguise of a single tax, has done the same thing in Kiao Chow that she has done in Poland. Of course, she has justified herself in doing this that "dadurch ist die Landspeculation im Schutzgebiet von jeder Betatigung zuruckgehaltenworden, under Stadt hast das Heft der Grund-und Boden-Politik in der Hand behalten."[2]

Main Characteristics of Kiao Chow under German Administration

It is in the characteristics of Kiao Chow that we see both Germany's strength and her inherent defects. On the one hand, Germany has practically Germanized the territory of Kiao Chow. A special commissioner for the engineer picturesquely says, "Everywhere, everything was German. The officials were German, the language was

---

[1] westm., vol. 70, pp. 17–21.
[2] Grotewold, Unser Kolonialwesen, p. 181.

German, and the coinage was German. All goods[①] not produced in Shantung were brought from Germany from a needle to an electric crane. There was no leakage and no exception. One remarkable thing is that pidgin German is unknown."[②]

But, in spite of the predominance of German civilization in KiaoChow, the territory is little more than billets for a number of officials and soldiers. In the statistics of 1913, there were 3,806 Germans out of the total white population in Kiao Chow but 2,638 of them were official persons, who comprised, two-thirds of the German population. The place is artificially created and artificially maintained and is governed by red tape. The policy is to secure immediate and direct advantage for the mother country. The German merchants find themselves treated by their own officials like recruits, in the hands of Prussian officers, of whom most are ignorant of commercial interests and have a fine contempt for trade.

So although the territory was under German administration, the smallness of Germany's trade in Kiao Chow was quite insignificant as compared with Japan in Dairen and England in Hong Kong. This is witnessed to in the trade of 1910:[③]

	Germany's share (L)	Total trade (L)	Percent of Total (%)
Imports	109, 000	3, 501, 000	3.1
Exports	17, 000	2, 369, 000	0.7

It is due to these reasons that Mr. Colquhoun[④] draws the conclusion

---

① This, however, is not quite true except in the Germans themselves. See p. 39.
② Journal of the American Asiatic Association, Jan. 1915, p. 365.
③ Hard and Castle, German Sea Power, p. 288.
④ Colquhoun, The Mastery of the Pacific, p.408.

that the Germans merchants, however enthusiastic they may be over the colonial policy, have hitherto shown a marked disinclination to settle or invest at Kiao Chow and that Mr. Hart[①] aptly remarks that the population is almost all military and official; genuine German colonists will not come out to Tsingtao on faith. Germany is surpassingly fitted for scientific colonization, but it is a pity that she has stood at the same time for other things which have tended to neutralize and obscure her success, and to cast ridicule upon the social sciences. This autocratic idea is certainly an inherent defect in the German system of national expansion. Kiao Chow would be far more flourishing if the German merchants might enjoy to the same degree of the most complete liberty, courtesy, and consideration in the treaty ports of China. German writers have been almost unanimous in condemning this bureaucracy but as the Kaiser says, "if we wish to accomplish anything in the world, the pen will be powerless to carry it out."

---

① Hart, The Obvious Orient, p. 226.

CHAPTER III

KWANTUNG

CHAPTER III KWANTUNG

Port Arthur, Talienwan① and the southern Liaotung Peninsula, comprising the Russian leased territory, combined under the name of the Province of Kwantung, are situated on the southernmost extremity of the Province of Shengking. This territory has an area of about 1,256 square miles, exclusive of a neutral zone② and the waters surrounding the leased territory. It was leased to Russia on March 26, 1898, and ruled under her administration until New Year's Day of 1905 when the Japanese received Russian General Stoessel's surrender of the whole territory. China's official recognition of the transfer was concluded in a treaty with Japan on December 22, 1905.

Kwantung has a distinct feature in the fact that unlike Kiao Chow: it has one port for naval operations and another for commercial transactions. It has Port Arthur for the purpose of the former and Talienwan for the latter.

The importance attached to Port Arthur as a naval base is surpassed by none in the Chinese waters. Its superb position is evidenced by the fact that in the Russo-Japanese War, it took the Japanese 156 days to capture it. So far as power of resistance in modern times is concerned, it stands second only to Sevastopol which took 327 days before its fall and to Przemysl which it recently took 200 days to capture.③ Port Arthur is the key to Manchuria as 203 Meter Hill is the key to Port Arthur. Its position is rendered more important by its nearness to Peking, the capital of China.

---

① Talienwan is also called Dalny or Dairen.
② The neutral zone is situated to the north of the boundary of the leased territory. Its northern boundary commences on the west coast of Liaotung at the mouth of the Kaichow River, passes north of Yu-Yen Chang to the Tayang River, and follows the left bank of that river to its mouth which is included in the neutral zone.
③ Outlook, March 31, 1915.

With respect to Talienwan, or Dairen, its rate of growth in commerce since the Japanese occupation surpasses all other ports even Kiao Chow. Mr. Langhome has every reason to justify his statement that it is the Southampton of the East.

In every respect the leased territory Kwantung stands first in importance except only that Kowloon ranks ahead of it by reason of the immense volume of commerce in Hong Kong. It controls the outlet of coal mines which according to 1913 are more than four times as rich as those in the hinterland of Kiao Chow. A network of 701 miles of railways, which in length is a little more than 2½ times the German system in Kiao Chow, is under the direct control of South Manchurian Railway Company and is in direct connection with both Dairen and Port Arthur while its connection with Peking, Seoul, Kalgan, Newchuang, Harbin, Vladivostok and the trans-Siberian Railway is far more immediate than the Tsinan-Kiao Chow system. Kwantung's mastery of the situation is certainly the most powerful and formidable.

Port Arthur, Talienwan and the Cassini Convention

In the Autumn of 1896, the world was startled by the publication of the Cassini Convention①, a memorandum filed by Cassini, the Russian Minister to Peking, with the Chinese government in proof form. It clearly shows the Russian intention in regard to Port Arthur and Talienwan. Article 10 says, "As the Liaotung ports of Lushunkow (Port Arthur), and Talienwan and their dependencies are important strategic

---

① For the whole text of the Convention see Weale's The Reshaping of the Far East, vol. 2, p. 439.

CHAPTER III KWANTUNG

points, it shall be incumbent upon China to properly fortify them with all haste and to repair all their fortifications, etc., in order to provide against future dangers; Russia shall, therefore, lend all necessary assistance in helping to protect these ports, and shall not permit any foreign power to encroach upon them. China, on her part, also binds herself never to cede them to another country, but if, in the future, the exigencies of the case require it, and Russia should find herself suddenly involved in a war, China consents to allow Russia temporarily to concentrate her land and naval forces within the said ports, in order the better to enable Russia to attack the enemy, or to guard her own position." There has been a long dispute, since its publication, as to whether it was simply a ballon d'essai or a permanent arrangement. The fact that it was denounced by both parties on account of premature publication was, however, by no means a proof that it was not in accord with Russia's real manipulations, though, as believed by best authorities, it was never ratified.

Port Arthur, Talienwan and Germany's Occupation of Kiao Chow

It has been pointed out in the second chapter that the Cassini Convention had hastened the German occupation of Kiao Chow; it is, however, no less true that the German occupation of Kiao Chow in turn hastened and made definite the realization of Russia's manipulation in Port Arthur, Talienwan and other places. When Germany suddenly put landing parties on shore and hoisted her flag over Kiao Chow Bay, the Russians were not only completely taken by surprise but in addition, they were very much enraged. A compromise must be made if disputes were to be avoided. It was when things were at this stage that one of those memorable meetings between the Kaiser and the Czar took place. How the compromise was made is seen in the simple language[①]:"We occupied Kiao Chow because we desired reparation and a coaling station. We understand that the Cassini Convention was simply a ballon d'essaiand not a permanent arrangement. A year and more had passed since its publication and denouncement, and you took no steps to carry out its main provisions. Therefore we were forced to the conclusion that you had reconsidered your position. It is perhaps best so. For we cannot and do not intend to retreat; We have important interests in the Far East which must be consolidated......Russia's true objectives are ice-free ports connected by rail with her own territory. Your strength is in your many millions, and your strength must be shown more on land than on sea. Take the end of the Liaotung Peninsula; connect Port Arthur and Talienwan with your trans-Manchuria, Baikal-Vladivostok Railway, by the straightest possible route, and you will be in a position you could never hope to occupy by seizing a detached lease as Kiao Chow." So in the words of Putman Veale, "The substitution in the Russian leasing agreement of a vigorous and definite language in place of the vague and irresolute phrasing of the Cassini instrument must be directly attributed to German influence and to the use of German models."

The Story of the Russian Occupation

With this mutual understanding, we find on December 18,1897, a month after the German occupation of Kiao Chow, three Russian war

---

① Weale, The Reshaping of the Ear East, vol.l, p.344.

CHAPTER Ⅲ KWANTUNG

vessels arrived at Port Arthur. Soon after the appearance of the Russian squadron, Admiral Buller of the British navy arrived at Temulpo with seven ships and ordered two ships to proceed to Port Arthur. This was however recalled on the protest from Russia. Four days later it was officially explained by Count Muravieff that the step taken was entirely a questions of convenience for the ships, and had absolutely no connection with the occupation of the Bay of Kiao Chow by the Germans. The Count further stated that though Port Arthur furnished many advantages for repairing and for freedom from ice in the winter yet Vladivostok was at present furnished with a powerful ice breaker and would remain as their centre in the Far East. England which at that time had more suspicions than any other country except China over the action which Russia had just taken, seized upon the declaration of the Russian Minister by demanding firmly the opening of Talienwan to foreign trade[①], a move which was, among other things, to forestall the possible Russian occupation of this port as well as Port Arthur. This struck at the root of the matter and made the Russians very indignant. So the Russian ambassador in London urged very strongly that if the British Government insisted on making Talienwan an open port, it would be encroaching on the Russian sphere of influence and denying Russia in the future that right to the use of Port Arthur to which the progress of events had given her a claim. At the same time, the Russian charge d'affaires told the Tsungli Yamen at Peking that if it constituted Talienwan as an open port, it would incur the hostility of Russia by doing so. England was thus obliged to sign the loan agreement without the Talienwan clause. But

---

① As a condition of a loan agreement between China and England.

Russia did not stop with the striding out of this clause; she boldly went a step further by bringing forward, on March 7, her long-cherished design of the lease of Port Arthur, Talienwan, and the railway concession from Petma on the Trans-Manchurian Railway to the ports on the pretext of equal rights with the German agreement which was concluded on March 6. England again protested that Port Arthur was not a commercial centre; England would not object to the Russian lease of an ice-free commercial harbor connected by rail with the Trans-Siberian Railway but questions of an entirely different kind were opened if Russia obtained control of a military port in the neighborhood of Peking. The Russians, however, cared nothing for these empty words. And she had her lease signed on the 27th of March.①

Government during the Russian Rule

By the regulation of 1899, the Kwantung government was placed under the jurisdiction of the Russian Ministry of war with its chief seat of administration at Port Arthur. The administration was headed by a governor, appointed and removed at the immediate will of the Czar, who was commander-in-chief of the army and navy forces in the Heilony River region, Port Arthur, and Vladivostok.

Talienwan being mainly open to foreign trade, its organization and administration were placed on a separate basis from the rest of Kwantung. An Imperial order was promulgated on July 30, 1899, ordering that near Talienwan a new town named Dalny should be created.

---

① Hertslet, China Treaties, vol. 1, p. 505.

By the provisional regulations of August 20, of the same year already referred to, the organization was assigned to the Chinese Eastern Railway Company under the chief direction of the Minister of Finance, and its administration was entrusted to a prefect, to be appointed and dismissed by Imperial orders and subordinated to the governor of Kwantung. In August 1903, however, new administrative arrangements were made; by which the Kwantung territory was combined with the Helongjiang Province to be formed into a special vice royalty. This existed until the Russo-Japanese War.

Provisions of Treaty with respect to Kwantung

In spite of a few differences, the provisions of the treaty with respect to the lease of Kwantung bear a general resemblance to the provisions of the German lease. The provisions of military, naval and civil administration within the leased territory, and the provisions of the relations between China and Russia within the neutral zone are materially the same as those concluded between China and Germany. Differences, however, are found in some places. First, should any criminal cases occur, the Chinese criminal is to be handed over to the nearest Chinese officials to be punished while in Kiao Chow, some special cases are subjected to German jurisdiction. Second, Port Arthur, unlike Kiao Chow, is solely a naval port, only Russian and Chinese vessels are to be allowed to use it, while Talienwan, with the exception of a part within the port which, like Port Arthur, is to be reserved for the use of Russian and Chinese men-of-war, is to continue port, where the merchant vessels of all countries can freely come and go. Third, railway concessions are explicitly inserted into the treaty while in the case of Kiao Chow they are only arranged by agreement. In addition to the provisions for the construction of the extended line from a point on the Chinese Eastern Railway to Talienwan, the agreement[①] of September 8, 1896, concluded between China and the Russo-Chinese Bank shall be strictly applied. This provision is significant for both commercial and strategical reasons. Among other things, the agreement provides that goods imported from Russia into China by rail and exported from China to Russia in the same manner, shall pay respectively an import or export duty to the extent of one-third less as compared with the duty imposed at Chinese seaport customs houses. This was originally intended to develop the commerce between China and Russia; as applied to Talienwan, it was also conducive to the development of Russian commerce in that port. But the worst of all is the eighth section, which provides that the preservation of order and decorum in the land assigned to the railway and its appurtenances shall be confided to police agents appointed by the company and the company shall, for this purpose, draw up and establish police regulations. The application of these two provisions would make Russia to be both commercial and military masters in the leased territory and the vicinity surrounding the railway line and its branches. Fourth, in Article V of an additional amendment between China and Russia, which was concluded on May 7, of the same year provides that without Russia's consent no road and mining concessions shall be made in the neutral territory while in Kiao Chow, this is extended to the whole province of

---

① A full text of the Russo-Manchurian agreement Railway is found in Weale's The Reshaping of the Far East, vol. 2, p. 444.

Shantung. Further, without Russia's consent use no concession will be granted on the neutral ground for the use of subjects of other powers. This is not found in the treaty relating to Kiao Chow. Finally, the term is fixed at 25 years instead of 99 years as is in the case of Kiao Chow. Unlike the Kiao Chow treaty, there is no provision for the return of the leased territory before the expiration of the term but for an extension after expiration by mutual agreement.

Talienwan under Russian Rule

As has been pointed out, part of this port was opened to trade according to treaty provisions. Although Russia put more emphasis on military and political undertakings in the territory of Kwantung, she, however, did not neglect its commercial importance. It was Mr. Witte's plan to create Talienwan as the commercial terminus of the great Siberian Railway, and eventually the mere an tile outlet on the Pacific of the vast Russian Empire. This is evidenced by the fact that before the Russo-Japanese War, the works at Dalny (Talienwan) , including its large docks and piers, had cost already nearly 20,000,000 rubles.[①]

During the Russian period, Talienwan was an open port, so there was no accurate data to show its commercial growth. The trade of Russia with Manchuria may, however, give a little idea about the trade condition in Talienwan:

---

① The equivalent of a ruble in American dollar is about fifty-one cents.

Date	Trade value in rubles
1900	56,000,000
1901	51,000,000
1902	38,000,000

From the above figures, we learn that the Russian trade in Manchuria appeared to be growing smaller. But this decline was due to the withdrawal of military traffic rather than due to the Russian method of conducting business. When Russia leased the territory, and opened Dalny as a free port, she did her best to promote her commerce there. By discrimination in transportation rates, and by preventing the collection of customs duties at Dalny, she attempted to divert to that port, where her own merchants were established, the trade formerly belonging to Newchwang which was the base of the commerce carried on in Manchuria by other nations. She also took measures to increase her own imports to the Manchurian provinces. Fourteen steamers, subsidized to the amount of $ 309,000 annually[1] were put in operation between European Russia, and Vladivostok, Port Arthur and Dalny. The system of advancing to Chinese merchants by the Russo-Chinese Bank , together with imports free of duty and favorable rates in export duties, had led Mr. Miller, the American consul, to urge that these were likely to enable Russian cotton to capture the great trade of Manchuria that was now largely in the hands of American manufacturers.[2] These conditions and other political considerations had caused the United States to demand in 1903 the opening of Mukden and Antung to

---

[1] U. S. Consular Reports, vol. 73, p. 40.
[2] Commercial China, 1904, p. 2383.

CHAPTER III KWANTUNG

international residence and trade and caused Japan with the support of England and the United States to demand the opening of Tatungkao for the same purpose in order to weaken Russia's influence.

It might be well, in this connection, to say a few words about American trade with Manchuria during this period. Manchuria, at this time, imported more goods from the United States than from any other foreign country, and American, imports at Newchwang between 1900–1904 amounted to about $ 5,000,000 annually.① In 1901, out of a total of $ 24,813,692 native and foreign imports at $ 14,660,000 represented cotton goods, and of this about one-third was American piece goods. In 1902, about thirty-five percent of the total foreign imports at Newchwang came from the United States, and the greater part of this was cotton goods. In 1903, the total foreign imports were $ 13,314,012, and America's share was $ 5,562,255, of which $ 4,873,960 was cotton goods. These figures will suffice to show the position held by the United States in former years in regard to the most important import of Manchuria. The Russians were able to produce cotton fabrics almost as good as the American goods, but the 5,000 miles trans-Siberian freight was twice as expensive as the Pacific transportation. So by far, the greater part of sheetings, drills, and jeans came from America. However, the prosperity only belonged to cotton goods. As to kerosene oil and wheat flour, we find a steady decrease since the Russian lease of Kwantung. The importation of American kerosene at Newchwang fell from 3,172,000 gallons in 1901 to 603,180 gallons in 1902; and American flour was almost driven from the market by the Russian mills at Harbin. But these articles made up only

---

① Annals of the American Academy, vol. 39–40, p.157.

a small part of the total trade, so it might be safe to say that during this period American trade conditions in Manchuria were very satisfactory in spite of the aggressive policy which the Russians followed.

Port Arthur under the Russian Rule

Port Arthur was the naval base as distinguished from Talienwan which was devoted mainly to trade. Russia refortified this port and made it into a great naval and military stronghold. From the time of the lease up to the Russo-Japanese War, fifty-nine permanent forts, including such famous forts as the 203-Metre Hill, Erlingshan and Signal Hill were built; 546 guns, including 54 of large calibre, were mounted; 5 great battleships, 14 gunboats, and some 50 small vessels were placed in this harbor. These actual undertakings have already shown to us how tremendous an energy Russia had put into the building up of Port Arthur.

Railway Concession under the Russian Lease

The treaty provided that Russia was allowed to extend the Chinese Eastern Railway to Talienwan. In order to understand the importance of this extension, it might be well to say a word about the original Chinese Eastern Railway. The construction of this railway together with the privilege of exploitation was conceded to the Russo-Chinese Bank in 1896. The main line[①]begins at a point on the trans-Siberian Railway, Manchowli, runs via Harbin and ends at Suifengho, the point of

---

① China's Year Book,1914, p.211 and p.234.

continuation of the trans-Siberian Railway to Vladivostok making a total of 921 miles. The extension starting from Harbin consists of 608 miles of which 439 miles from Changchun to Port Arthur are later known as the South Manchurian Railway after having been transferred to Japan. It was stipulated in the original agreement that the line was to be the property of the Chinese Eastern Railway Company for eighty years upon the expiration of which time reverted to China without cost. It also provided for the purchase of the line 36 years after it was put in operation at a price representing the cost of the line and interest. These provisions apply to the extension line.

  The construction of the line was pushed ahead rapidly and by the beginning of the Boxer outbreak, with the exception of a number of bridges, it was practically finished. During the Boxer trouble, much of the line was destroyed and especially the extension which is between Port Arthur and Harbin. The work was, however, renewed with vigor and in the fall of 1901, the Chinese Eastern Railway together with the extension was completed. The entire system cost 150,000,000 out of which sum $55,000,000 was used in the construction of the extension line. This is exclusive of the 250, 000, 000 rubles spent in the building up of Port Arthur, Dalny and other enterprises outside the strict railway expenditures.

  This railway is of utmost importance. It connects Kwantung with Manchuli, Vladivostok, Harbin, the so-called Moscow of China, then Saint Petersburg by way of the trans-Siberian Railway, and finally with Peking through the Peking-Mukden Railway. An article in the *Far Eastern Review* for May 1909 says, "This was the link which was to bind the Pacific literal with the great trans-Siberian Railway, through Chinese territory in northern Manchuria, thus avoiding the greater task of following the crooked Helong River in the endeavor to seek an outlet to the sea. At the same time, it created a new line of attack and approach to the goal of Peking." So not only the Point of Regent Sword (Port Arthur) was under its influence but the whole of Manchuria and the National Capital was at stake.

And finally, the building of the railway carried with it the right of mining in regions both along the railway and dependent of the railway, and also the privilege of guarding the railway. The cost of policing the railway alone had been 24,000,000 rubles, or $12,000,000, policemen were soldiers and soldiers were policemen. This military police force along the railway had been found to be most effective in carrying out Russia's underhanded plan.

The Russo-Japanese Conflict

It was unfortunate for Russia that she was not the only one who looked toward Kwantung. Her plan was magnificent but her adversary was also pressing. The fact that Russia took an active part in the retrocession of the Liaotung Peninsula to China and again tried to lease it from China for herself was a thing that Japan never forgot.

For Japan's expansion into the said territory was more natural and more urgent than Russia's. Her population from 1828 up to the Russo-Japanese War had almost doubled. In 1828, Japan had only a population of 27,000,000; in 1875, of 34,000,000 and in 1904, of 47,000,000.[①] The growth of

---

[①] K. Asakawa, The Russo-Japanese Conflict, p. 2. According to 1910, the Japanese population has increased to 50,984,000. During the six years between 1904 to 1910, Japan's annual increase in population has been seven-tenths million.

population is one of the most important factors that caused Japan's expansion to conflict with Russian interests.

Further, the development of Japan seemed to lie in the direction of industry and trade rather than agriculture. Less than 13, 000, 000 acres of land or 13% of the extent of the whole country were under-cultivation at that time while the arable area of the land cannot be possibly increased by more than 10, 500, 000 acres. It is evident that the per capita share of the arable land is even less than the corresponding rate in England and less than half of that in China. The tenants live from hand to mouth and cannot always afford even the necessary fertilizers and the proprietor's profit hardly rises above 5% while the capital employed pays an interest of 15% to 30%. This condition has directed the Japanese mainly into commercial channels. So her trade with foreign countries increased from 49, 742, 831 yen in 1873 to 606, 637, 959 yen in 1903. Manchuria was then considered by far the most important place for her commercial expansion; in order for the Japanese trade to flourish in the Manchurian market, it was thought very desirable to have control of its gateway.

Finally, the Japanese have fed themselves with the same national delusion as other ambitious nations. They believe that in order to become a great power they must not hesitate to seize territory at the expense of others. They believe that the greatness of Japan must lie in her domination over the Continent. Imperialism means Continentalism and Continentalism must be accomplished by Militarism.

These urgent factors together with the intolerable aggression of Russia in Korea and in Manchuria rendered a war inevitable. Japan seemed to be silent at the retrocession of Liaotung but her long preparation for the war was too obvious if we examine the following budget:

Date	Total expenditure (yen)	Military expenditure (yen)	%
1894–5	78,128,000	20,662,000	26.4
1895–6	85,317,000	23,536,000	27.6
1896–7	168,856,000	73,248,000	43.4
1897–8	223,678,000	110,542,000	49.3
1898–9	219,757,000	112,427,000	51.1
1899–0	254,165,000	114,212,000	44.9
1900–1	292,750,000	133,113,000	45.4
1901–2	266,856,000	102,360,000	38.3
1902–3	289,226,000	85,768,000	29.7
1903–4	244,752,000	71,368,000	31.7
1904–5	223,181,000	69,433,000	31.1

From the above table, we notice the sudden increase in Japan's army and navy expenditure after 1896; we notice that from 1896 to 1905 the army and navy covers an average of 40% of the total expenditure. She prepared for the war for nine years. She prepared for the war because she thought war was the only means which would enable her to get control over Kwantung—the gateway to Manchuria and eventually the gate-way to her Continental Policy. On the other hand, an ice-free port such as Port Arthur and Talienwan linked with her vast empire was considered as an absolute necessity for Russian expansion. So both nations had vital interests at stake; both nations were fully prepared for a struggle, and both nations believed that the settlement of this dispute could be found only in war. This began on the night of February 8, 1904.

Transfer of Kwantung to Japan

It is not in the scope of this paper to discuss the war between Japan and Russia. In a word, the war has settled the dispute over this territory and other things at least for the time being. By the treaty of Portsmouth, Russia agreed, among other things, to transfer Kwantung and the railway and mining rights to Japan, provided China would consent thereto. A conference was called between Japan and China subsequently. Although no outward friction developed at the conferences, it was well known that China acceded to the treaty with great reluctance, especially in the matter of the transfer of Kwantung to Japan. China would have preferred to have rescinded this obnoxious lease together. But she was not successful and a treaty[①] between China and Japan was concluded on December 22, 1905, whereby the Chinese Imperial government consented to all transfers and assignments by Russia to Japan by articles V and VI of the treaty of peace.[②]

Kwantung under Japan Rule

According to the Imperial Japanese Ordinances relating to the administration of Kwantung and the offices subordinate to it, issued on September 1, 1906, the Governor-generalship is to be filled with either a Lieutenant-General or Full-General with the highest official ranks accorded to him. The Governor-General governs Kwantung Province, has command of the troops under him and directs administration,

---

① Hertslet, China Treaties, vol. 1, p, 392.
② Ibid,p. 610. Article V refers to the transfer of the lease of Kwantung; article VI refers to the transfer of the Changchun–Port Arthur Railway and of coal mines.

subject to the supervision of the Minister of Foreign Affairs. The Governor-General is authorized under a special commission to conduct negotiations with the Chinese local authorities; he shall receive the instructions of the Minister of War and the Chief of the General Staff and the Inspector General of Military Education in matters relative to the military administration and personnel.

Port Arthur after the Transfer

The importance of this port as a military and naval base has been touched upon in the former paragraphs. Riojun, as the Japanese call it, is now the headquarters of the Japanese civil and military administration in the province of Kwantung. The town is divided into two parts, the old, and the new. The forts and harbors built by the Russians are repaired and more fully and adequately equipped. On July 1, 1910[①], the western harbor was thrown open to the ships of all nations with a view to fostering international trade; or better to fostering Japanese trade. With the opening of the Dairen–Port Arthur Branch Railway, the journey between these two ports occupies only one hour and a half by train. This will allow the military authority at Port Arthur more readily to exert influence on helping to promote Japanese trade at Dairen.

Dairen after the Transfer

The name Dairen itself begins with the transfer. This port was

---

① Directory and Chronicle for China, p.818.

CHAPTER III KWANTUNG

formerly called Talienwan and Dalny. The most distinguished feature that characterizes Dairen as soon as the transfer was made was the fact that Japan uses her governmental and military control of the place to get everything worth having while her regulations kept competitors out. The purpose of the government respecting trade in Kwantung and Manchuria as printed in newspapers, is summed up by Mr. Millard in four articles, as follows:[①]

Article 1. The government to guarantee a loan of 6,000,000 yen at 4%, to be advanced to Japanese merchants doing business in Manchuria (Including Kwantung), to assist them in establishing trade for Japanese goods.

Article 2. The Japanese goods destined for Manchuria to be delivered upon credit under certain limitations.

Article 3. The South Manchurian Railway Company to carry such goods free, or at half the usual rate, for one year.

Article 4. Maritime freightage in Japanese ships carrying Japanese goods to Manchuria to be free, or at half the usual rate, for one year.

Mr. Millard further says that no duties are being charged on Japanese goods imported from Japan.

This sharp discrimination, however, did not last very long because it led the Diplomatic Corps at Peking to urge that steps be taken to have the Chinese Customs House established at Dairen which has formed a customs district under the Chinese Imperial Fort since July 1, 1907[②], with arrangements the same as those at Kiao Chow.[③] Dairen is the chief

---

① Millard, America and the Far Eastern Questions, p. 191.
② China's Year Book, 1914, p.120.
③ See Chapter II. This arrangement has removed the tariff discrimination at Dairen but Japanese products which reach Korea through Gensan are brought into Manchuria by way of Chientao without duty being paid although this route is more expensive.

customs district but it is not the only customs district in Kwantung. It has outstations at Kinchow, Pulantien, Pitzemo, and Port Arthur.

Dairen is recognized as the most rapidly growing port in modern China, and it is worthwhile to notice its volume of trade during recent years.

Date	Imports in hk.tls.	Exports in hk.tls.
1908	17, 215, 936	7, 342, 402
1909	12, 239, 563	22, 318, 144
1910	18, 671, 515	20, 183, 290
1911	24, 012, 724	24, 184, 154

From the above table, we learn that the trade at Dairen is exceedingly prosperous. But prosperity belongs to only one nation. Although Germany, Great Britain and Belgium have shown a little increase in their trade at Dairen, all the rest have suffered severely, and worst of all is the trade condition of the United States in this territory. A glance at the following table will give us some idea of the situation.[①]

During the period, from 1908 up to 1911, Kwantung's imports from Japan have nearly doubled while that from the United States have decreased by over 93 percent. It is curious to notice that in spite of the temporary decline in the total imports to Kwantung in 1909[②], Japan's imports to this territory showed an increase of two hundred thousand hk.tls. In 1911 more than three-fourths of the total imports and exports were in the hand of the Japanese. It is true that cheaper labor, cheaper cost of production and cheaper rate of transportation have made the situation more favorable to Japan yet Mr. Weale is justified in saying that Manchuria is practically

---

① Berichte,Deutsches Handels, Archive 1912, Part 2, P.642.
② See the first table of this page.

a closed market when we consider discrimination in rates of railway transportation and the delay of fixing trains for goods other than Japanese.

A Study of the Population in Kwantung and Manchuria

From the year 1908 to 1913, a period of six years, the number of Japanese in South Manchuria has nearly doubled. This overwhelming immigration is not only a matter of natural movement but also a policy developed by conscious efforts. The Japanese population in Manchuria is seen in the following table[①]:

Date	Number of Japanese
1908	46,942
1909	53,906
1910	62,338
1912	73,568
1913	82,978

According to the census of 1913, these Japanese immigrants are distributed, among the following places in Manchuria[②]:

Location	Number of Japanese
Kwantung	47,162
Mukden	13,969
Changchun	6,208
Antung	6,878
Newchwang	6,358
Harbin	1,413
Kirin & Tsi-tsihar	990

① The Japan Year Book, 1914, p. 713 and p. 39.
② Ibid, p. 38.

The situation will be more clearly perceived when we make a comparison of the Chinese and Japanese populations in Dairen and Port Arthur, the two principal cities in Kwantung. This comparison is here presented[①]:

Location	Japanese	Chinese
Dairen	29,395	20,338
Port Arthur	9,637	8,222

The writer has not found any other place in China where the aliens exceed the natives, except at Port Arthur, Dairen, and Harbin where the Russians are in the majority.

This constant pouring-in of Japanese population has both economical and political ends in view, but its effects do not stop here, and its influence tends to be detrimental to the already existing moral order. An English missionary, is quoted by Mr. Millard as saying[②], "I am very much disappointed at some results of the Japanese immigration... and the presence of thousands of Japanese men of low character and immoral women who openly ply their avocation in the streets of cities and towns, are corrupting influences new to the country, or only felt before in a limited degree." However, it must be admitted that such a statement is by no means true in all cases and many of the Japanese immigrants are satisfactory at least so far as private life is concerned.

Finance in Kwantung

The financial condition in Kwantung is very misleading at the first

---

① The Japan Year Book, 1914, p. 713.
② Millard, America and the Far Eastern Questions, p. 222.

glance at the budget. The budget excludes military expenses on the one hand, and the profit of the South Manchurian Railway Company on the other, which must be taken into consideration if we wish to have a clear idea of the financial condition in Kwantung.[①]

The ordinary revenue of Kwantung is drawn from taxes, public undertakings, state property, revenue stamps and miscellaneous receipts. Public undertaking and state property form the greatest items in ordinary revenue, which are estimated to be 1,626,000 yen or more than four-fifths of the total ordinary revenue in the budget of 1914-15. The extraordinary revenue consists mainly of the proceeds from the sale of state property and of appropriations from the central treasury. The first consists largely of lands transferred by the Russians and bought from the Chinese. The total extent of land (in Manchuria as well as in Kwantung, belonging to the South Manchurian Railway Company) is 70.54 square miles or 45,156 acres. So far as the public lands of Kwantung are concerned, its annual sales are given as follows:

Date	Value (Yen)
1908–09	1,200
1909–10	1,200
1910–11	17,616
1911–12	18,000
1912–13	777,000
1913–14	10,000
1914–15	26,000

① The Japan Year Book, 1908–09, p.573; 1910, p.633; 1912, p.662; 1913, p.683; 1914, p.714.

The annual Home Treasury subvention has been from 2,307,000 yen to 3,964,000 yen. The total revenue according to the budget of 1914–15 is 4,437,000 yen.

With regard to expenditure, the largest items in the budget of 1914–15 are communication expenses, being 1,050,000 yen, police and prison expenses, being 910,000 yen, etc. These make a total expenditure of 4,437,000 yen.

The point the writer wants to get at is that the 4,437,000 revenue against the 4,437,000 yen expenditure does not represent the true financial condition here.

In regard to expenditure, the navy in Kwantung and Manchurian waters in 1913–1914 costs 966,000 yen and the garrison in said regions cost Japan 4,660,000 yen. An expenditure of 5,500,000 yen is not so small a sum as to be neglected.

The 5,566,000 yen for military expenses, being entirely supported by the government, together with the Home Treasury subvention of the same year （1913–14）, makes a total expenditure of 8,674,000 yen. Now Japan is not a rich country. How can she do this year after year? She has no capital at hand but she has a machine to manufacture it. She has a South Manchurian Railway Company. This company yielded in the fiscal year of 1913–14 a net profit of 7,167,000 yen. This sum has practically covered all the expenses which Japan has incurred in Kwantung and Manchuria, and it is believed that this company will yield an ever-increasing profit to offset governmental expenditures, It is true that the profits are distributed not wholly in the payment of dividends to government shares but one must confess that the company is run by the government, its officials are appointed by the government and its

CHAPTER III KWANTUNG

profits must be dealt with as a part of national finance rather than a private gain. It is further true that the garrisons and navy in Manchurian waters are not solely for the protection of Kwantung, and that the South Manchurian Railway Company manages things not only in Kwantung but also in the entire South Manchuria, but the situation is such that Japan's manipulation in Manchuria is for Kwantung, and that in Kwantung is for Manchuria; the financial conditions in the two being so intermingled together and so complex that it is absolutely impossible to treat the one without taking the other into consideration. So the actual finances of Kwantung and Manchuria are given in the following table:

I. Receipts

Date	General revenue (yen)	Subvention (yen)	Net profit of S.M.R. (yen)
1907-08	4, 386, 000	3, 000, 000	1, 087, 988
1908-09	4, 653, 602	3, 120, 000	7, 375, 734
1909-10	4, 879, 489	3, 964, 000	
1910-11	4, 867, 988	3, 615, 000	7, 161, 000
1911-12	4, 984, 926	3, 643, 000	4, 928, 000
1912-13	5, 246, 000	3, 122, 000	4, 926, 000
1913-14	5, 739, 000	3, 047, 000	7, 167, 000
1914-15	4, 437, 000	2, 307, 000	

II. Expenditure

Date	General Expenditure (yen)	Garrison ExPenditure (yen)	Navy expenditure (yen)
1907-08	4, 386, 293		
1908-09	4, 653, 802		

续表

Date	General Expenditure (yen)	Garrison ExPenditure (yen)	Navy expenditure (yen)
1909–10	4,879,489	5,713,000	1,115,000
1910–11	4,867,988	5,296,000	1,091,000
1911–12	4,984,926	5,009,000	1,167,000
1912–13	5,246,000	4,497,000	1,095,000
1915–14	5,697,000	4,660,000	966,000
1914–15	4,437,000		

The South Manchurian Railway Company

After the South Manchurian Railway between Changchun, Dairen, and Port Arthur had been transferred to the Japanese government by Russia[①] with the consent of China, a company named Minami Manshu Tetsudo or South Manchurian Railway Company was organized by an Imperial decree to operate this line. By June 1906, the establishment of this company was formally announced. The organization committee held its first meeting on August 10, 1906. It was then considered a private company of a special character, but on April 1, 1907, the Field Railway Office formally transferred the railways and all belonging to the company. The control of the railways was transferred to the Minister of Communications in July 1908, and subsequently to the Imperial Railway Board.

With respect to the distribution of shares, the Organization Committee, during the first meeting of 1906, decided that the company should be

① The transfer took place on August 1, 1906.

capitalized at 200, 000, 000 yen, the government to receive 100,000,000 yen in shares for (1) railways already constructed[①], (2) all properties accessory to the above railways[②] and (3) coal mines at Fushun and Yentai[③]. The remaining shares were offered to Japanese and Chinese objects. The Chinese, however, failed to avail themselves of the opportunity to purchase shares.[④] The company raised a loan of £ 8, 000, 000 in 1908 in Europe, and the capital actually paid in by the shareholders was only 2,000,000 yen. In January 1911, a foreign loan of 60, 000, 000 yen was floated in London, 20, 000, 000 yen to repay the short-term loan, and the rest for reconstructing the Antung–Mukden Railway.[⑤] It is curious to notice how Japan works her way foreign capital. For the investment, the government further guarantees a profit of 6%.[⑥]

Such is the history and the capitalization of the South Manchurian Railway Company. But is it only a railway company?

In its administrative system, we find that the government reserves the right of appointing members of the administrative body, except the auditors who are elected for three years at the general meeting of shareholders. The term of the president and vice president is five years, and that of directors is four. Although the government must select them from among shareholders of at least 50 shares, yet beyond this limitation, the government has sole control over its administration. So viewed from its relations to the central government, the company is not only a

---

① Excluding the railway stock now in use, rails of the Mukden light railway and accessories.
② Excluding the property in the leased territory.
③ The Far Eastern Review, 1909, Nov. No., p. 288.
④ Ibid, p. 289.
⑤ The Japan Year Book, 1912, p. 664.
⑥ Ibid, p. 669.

business corporation but also a governmental agent.

With respect to the functions the company performs, the company controls not only the railways but all sorts of business. It engages in mining, marine transport, harbor business, houses, and electric and gas work. It sells on consignment the principal goods carried by rail. It controls the construction and administration of land and houses on the land belonging to the railways. It is empowered to make the necessary provisions for education, health, and engineering works within the limits of the land belonging to the railways. It is also entrusted to collect fees from the inhabitants within this region to defray the expenses of above. So, from its true nature and scope, the company is not only a railway company but also a colonial administrator. Besides the policing power which is under the supervision of the Kwantung Governor General, and the judicial power which belongs to the Consul, within this region, the South Manchurian Company is able to do anything.

Japanese Railways within and in connection with Kwantung

Japanese railways within and in connection with Kwantung under the direct control of the South Manchurian Railway Company consist of two lines: (1) the Changchun–Dairen line and its branches which have been transferred by Russia, and (2) the Antung–Mukden Railway of which the right of control has been given by the agreement between China and Japan. Besides these, there are two other lines, named the Changchun–Kirin Railway and the Simmintun–Mukden Railway of which half of the capital is borrowed from Japan but the control is vested in the hand of the Chinese.

CHAPTER III KWANTUNG

At the end of 1913, other attempts had been made by Japan for the construction of a network of railways in South Manchuria.

The Changchun-Dairen line, being transferred by Russia, consists of 439.5 miles. It opened to traffic in 1907. Besides this 439.5 miles, it has many branches: one branch is known as the Suchiatun-Fushun Collieries, consists of 34.5 miles; the second branch, Tashikiao-Yinkow, 13.5 miles, and finally, the Choushuitze-Port Arthur line, 31.5 miles. These are all of the standard gauges. The administration of this main line and its branches is based on the original agreement between China and the Russo-Chinese Bank, concluded in 1896. It is to be the property of the South Manchurian Railway Company for the remaining years of the eighty years, dated from the operation of the Chinese Eastern Railway, upon the expiration of which time it reverts to China without cost. If China should wish to purchase the line before its expiration, she can do so after the line has been put into operation for 36 years by paying a price representing the cost of the line and interest.

The Antung-Mukden Railway came into existence to meet the existence of the Russo-Japanese War, and was therefore hurriedly constructed. Subsequently, under article VI of the additional agreement between Japan and China dated December 22, 1905[1], Japan was given the privilege of improving and operating the Antung-Mukden line for a period of 15 years from the date of the agreement, after which the Chinese government acquired the right to purchase the line at the price determined by valuation and arbitration. The Japanese, however, construed improvement as reconstruction, and proceeded to relocate

---

[1] Hertslet, China Treaties, vol. 1, p. 395.

the line, and change its gauge. This is both a violation of the agreement and a blow at the Open Door Doctrine. Mr. Rea says, "It is significant that not one official protest was raised by any of the powers against Japan's move. The two powers professing the greatest adherence to the Open Door Doctrine, Great Britain and America, were conspicuous by their silence and apparent acquiescence in Japan's action."[①]

This line, consisting of 162 miles, was formerly under the control of the military authorities until its transfer to the South Manchurian Railway Company, in December of 1906. It was opened to traffic in August 1908.[②] Its conversion into broad gauge was completed by November 11, 1908.

These two lines with branches constitute a total millage of 701 miles. They traverse one of the richest areas in the world. Their connections with Korea, Siberia, and North China have made Japan the master of the situation.

In this connection, it might be well to say a word about the attitude which the United States took toward these railways and the Russian system in Manchuria. Since the Chinese Eastern Railway and the South Manchurian Railway furnish the gravest danger of future conflict, the United States in 1910, undertook to propose the neutralization of these two systems. But the plan failed to be carried through because both Japan and Russia strongly objected to it.

The third and fourth lines left for our discussion are the Changchun–Kirin Railway and the Sinmintun–Mukden Railway. The Changchun–Kirin Railway is 80 miles long. These two lines are under the direct

---

① The Far Eastern Review, Nov. 1909, p. 295.
② Ibid, p. 296.

CHAPTER Ⅲ　KWANTUNG

control of the Chinese government, but owing to the Japanese influence over them, something must be said if we wish to have a clear idea of the situation.

Prior to 1907, the Sinmintun–Mukden Railway was run by the Japanese. As this line forms a part of the Peking–Mukden Railway, it is of vital importance if China herself could have control over it. So by the treaty of April 15, 1907[①], the Chinese government purchased the Sinmintun–Mukden Railway by paying 1,990,000 yen, and on the following conditions:

1. The Chinese government in constructing the railway east of Liao (part of the Sinmintun-Mukden line), and the railway between Changchun and Kirin, shall borrow half of the funds from the South Manchurian Railway Company. The term of redemption of the loan shall be 18 years with regard to the loan relating to the Sinmintun–Mukden Railway east of the Liao, and 25 years with regard to the loan relating to the Kirin–Changchun Railway.[②]

2. With respect to the future extension of the Changchun–Kirin Railway, in case of China lacking funds, Japan shall be asked for the loan unless China can construct on her own account, thus eliminating all other countries to compete with Japan.

3. During the term of loan, Japanese shall be engaged as chief engineers and railway accountants.

4. Receipts of the above railways shall be deposited with Japanese banks.

5. Both the Sinmintun–Mukden and Kirin–Changchun Railways to

---

① Hertslet, China Treaties, vol. 1, p. 397.
② The term begins with the date of opening, i.e. Oct. 20, 1912.

be constructed by China shall be connected with the South Manchurian Railway.

Mining in Manchuria

Next in importance to railways is the privilege of mining. It is not only advantageous for its annual profit but also for its being a basis of a sphere of influence.

The Fushun Collieries[①] situated about 22 miles east of Mukden and contain deposits from 80 to 175 feet in thickness. The storage is estimated to be at least 800 million tons. Seven pits are now in operation with the total daily output of 3,000 tons.

The Yentai coal fields exist north of Liaoyang and can be reached in an hour by rail from the Yentai station. The daily output is 100 tons.

The annual estimate of coal production of these two mines is as follows:

Date	Output (tons)	Net profit (yen)
1911	1,382,000	2,628,000
1912	1,513,000	1,846,000
1913	2,281,000	1,800,000

In order to facilitate transportation, two branches of railways have been built to connect these coal fields with the South Manchurian Railway. The Fushan branch consists of 38.9 miles and the Yentai branch, 9.7 miles. Both branches opened in 1908.

---

① The Japan Year Book, 1913, p. 688; 1914, p. 716.

CHAPTER III KWANTUNG

Russia in Manchuria after the War of 1904

It is true that Japan gains influence in Manchuria at the expense of Russia. But did Russia's influence disappear with the war? Did Russia ever forgotten the war? In fact, Russia's influence is still felt in two-thirds of Manchuria, including the entire northern watershed, embracing the region drained by the Sungari and its tributaries; she controls jointly with Manchuria the mighty Helang Riven; she has a Manchurian and the trans-Siberian Railways fortified seaport in Vladivostok connected with Siberia and European Russia by the Manchurian and the trans-Siberian Railways; her hold in Mongolia is not materially weakened; while behind it and beyond it always stands her massive empire. Her position in Manchuria is defined by the Portsmouth Treaty and, in an international sense, is identical with Japan. The northern railways are policed by Russian guards. Russian garrison are found at Tsitsihar, Mongar, Aigun, Sangsan, Urga and several other places near Manchuria. Although her grip is not so tight as the Japanese, her immigration into Manchuria, after the war up to 1908, has trebled, being 180,000 in 1906, 400,000 in 1907, and 500,000 in 1908. She owns 8 flour mills in Manchuria with a total daily output of 47,000 poods. Everything has been done for the military provision and unexpected emergencies.① Certainly she has not forgotten the humiliating result of the war of 1904, Japan too has not neglected to note that Russia has not abandoned her secret plan of revanche. So with Mr. Millard, "A greater Japan will mean the knell of Russia's Eastern Policy; a greater Russia in the East may make impossible Japan's eventual supremacy there. Between the two greater, China will solve the questions itself by maintaining international equilibrium in the Far East."

---

① Russian flour mills in Manchuria are given as follows:

Location	Daily output in poods
Sungari	10,000
Zozulingsky	7,000
Manchu	6,000
Druzen	2,000
Riff	3,000
Nowalski	7,000
Turkim	10,000
Klondineff	1,000

CHAPTER IV

KWANG CHOW WAN

CHAPTER IV KWANG CHOW WAN

Kwang Chow Wan (or according to the French official spelling, Kouang-tcheou-wan) , the French leased territory, is situated at a distance of 230 miles from Hong Kong, W. S · W. on the coast of the province of Kwangtung.① It comprises an area of 190 square miles. This includes the two islands which were added to it in 1899.② The treaty was signed between China and France on 27th May, 1898, and is materially the same as the German treaty of Kiao Chow.③

Administration of Kwang Chow Wan

Following the convention of delimitation signed on the 16th of November,1899, between Marshal Sou and Admiral Courrejolles, the territory of Kwang Chow Wan was placed under the authority of the Governor-General of Indo-China.④ The territory has been divided into three administrative circumscriptions, but the Chinese communal organization is maintained.⑤

Fort Bayard as a Port

The chief place of the territory is the town of Fort Bayard, which

---

① Directory and Chronicle for China, 1914, p,1082.
② The Statesman's Year Book, 1906, p.877.
③ Hertshet, China Treaties, p.328.
④ French Indo-China consists of five states: Anam, Cambodia, Cochin China, Tonkin and Laos. The whole country is under a Governor-General, assisted by a Secretary-General and each of the states has its head, a functionary called Resident Superior except in Cochin China which has a governor at its head.
⑤ The Statesman's Year Book, 1914, p.851.

is at the entrance of the interior port on the right bank of the river Ma Teche. It is the commercial centre of this leased territory. Kwang Chow Wan is understood to be a free port in which all commercial operations can be carried on without paying any duty. "Governor Dourner has expressed the hope that the absence of customs duties and the entire liberty allowed to ships of commerce will tend to make it soon one of the principal entrepots of the Far East."① Commerce has already largely extended. In 1912, the imports and exports of Kwang Chow wan were estimated to be 8,412,875 Piasters,② or $3,600, 000.

Kwang Chow Wan as a Naval Base

The two islands of Naochow and Tanghai placed at the entrance of the bay make it an excellent closed port, into which entrance is through two narrow passages. Mr. Morse says, "The Bay has a good anchorage, but with a difficult entrance through sandy banks."③ Barracks are built on river Ma Teche. On the whole, Kwang Chow Wan is the least valuable naval base among the five.

Finance in Kwang Chow Wan

There is no adequate statement to be found about finance in Kwang Chow Wan. The local budget for 1914 balanced at 323,000 Piasters or $150,000 which is about equal to that in Wei Hai Wei.

---

① Reinsch, Colonial Administration, pp.245–246.
② The Statesman's Year Book,1914, p.849. The equivalent of a Piaster is about 24d.
③ Morse, The Trade and Administration of China, p.268.

Railway Concessions in Connection with the Lease of Kwang Chow Wan

With the concession of the right of railway construction secured in the treaty of lease, the French government entrusted the work to the Sociétie de Construction des Chemins de Fer Indo Chinosis. The total length of the line from Laokai to Yunnan is about 287 miles. It was opened to traffic in 1910. This line is connected with the Laokai-Haiphong railway which, consisting of 248 miles, will connect Yunnanfu with the sea and will possibly make Haiphong the terminal of southwestern China. France conquered Tonkin with the fixed idea of gaining ready commercial and political access to China throughput Yunnan province. This is why she exerts her best energy[1] in constructing the Tonkin-Yunnanfu railway, Her engineers have strenuously determined to overcome the 1600-meter ascent from the level of the Red River to the Yunnan plateau while her financiers incurred a total cost of $ 32, 216, 000 or an average cost of something over 60, 000 per mile.[2] The fact that the French are increasing their army in Indo-China aroused nother great suspicions in the mind of the Chinese Foreign Office as to their object and the Office has negotiated with the French Minister for a definite agreement that neither China nor France should station troops along the Yunnan-Tonkin Railway and that the Chinese section should be guarded by the Chinese police only. The Office in 1909 wired to the Viceroy of Yunnan to train the soldiers in his province in case

---

[1] The Far Eastern Review, 1909, Nov. No., p.303.
[2] Ibid p.304.

of emergency. So here again are planted the seeds for future trouble to China over a commercial concession originally given up to "cement the ties of friendship" with France.

Some Characteristics of Kwang Chow Wan

It was Bismark who described the colonial affairs of the three countries in the epigram, "England has colonies and colonists; Germany has colonists but no colonies; France has colonies but no colonists, Germany has colonists but no colonies; France has colonies but no colonists." This is the case in Kwang Chow Wan as well as in Indo-China. In spite of the reforms of Mr. Doumer, which have accomplished so much in the direction of improving the administration of Indo-China and Kwang Chow Wan, these places are still sparsely colonized.

CHAPTER V

WEI HAI WEI

CHAPTER V WEI HAI WEI

Wei Hai Wei, an English leased territory, which lies in latitude 37.30 N, longitude 122.10 E. on the north-east coast of the Shantung peninsula. It comprises the island of Luikung, all the islands in the Bay of Wei Hai Wei, and a belt of land ten miles wide along the entire coastline. The total area is 285 square miles, exclusive of a neutral zone of 1,505 square miles. It was leased to Great Britain by China by a convention signed at Peking, on the 1st of July, 1898.[①]

From its geographical position, Mr.Denby[②] says, "Wei Hai Wei is an excellent harbor, much larger and better than Port Arthur.[③] It is exactly at the mouth of the Gulf of Pechili, and is the nearest point on the Gulf to Korea. It commands the Gulf. It is about 40 miles from Chefoo and 80 miles from Kiao Chow. It is supposed here that it will be a second or northern Hong Kong."[④]

Viewed from its strategical importance, Charles Beresford says, "I consider it an immense acquisition to our naval strength in the China seas, as with but a comparatively small expenditure of money it could be made a most efficient and powerful naval base."[⑤] Again, he says, "At this moment there is no place in Chinese water where battleships can anchor so close to the shore."[⑥] However, Beresford admits that at present (1898), Wei Hai Wei is in no way to be compared in power to Port Arthur.

Commercially, it is an easy place for shipping to make. But as far

---

① Hertslet, China Treaties, vol.1, p.122.
② Presidential Messages and Foreign Relations of the U. S. 1898, p.190.
③ This is, however, not yet shown in fact.
④ It is still to be realized.
⑤ Charles Beresford, The Break-up of China, p.71.
⑥ Ibid, p.72.

as railway facilities are concerned, it is unlikely Wei Hai Wei can ever become a great mercantile port.

The Occupation of Wei Hai Wei[①]

As Great Britain failed to persuade Russia in dropping her demands for the lease of Port Arthur and Talienwan, and as Russia's lease of these ports together with Germany's lease of Kiao Chow were thought to be detrimental to British commercial safety in North China, she definitely resolved, on March 25, 1898 to demand speedily the lease of Wei Hai Wei. On April 3, the British fleet in Hong Kong was ordered to proceed to the Gulf of Peichili. It must be understood that Wei Hai Wei at that time was still in the hands of the Japanese who occupied it during the Chino-Japanese war. It was Japan's ambition, if possible to retain her control over it. But owing to the aggressive policy of the Russians and Germans in the North China Sea, Japan could not stand it without an alliance. The fact that Japan did not raise any objection against the English lease of Wei Hai Wei was because she had another object in view and that object was to have a defensive alliance with Great Britain. So the transfer of the territory went smoothly and was then put under the control of the admiralty of Great Britain.

---

① The Japan Weekly Mail, 1898.

CHAPTER V   WEI HAI WEI

Administration of Wei Hai Wei[①]

The administration, of Wei Hai Wei, was first undertaken by the Senior Naval Officer on the station in 1898. In the following year it was transferred to a military and civil commissioner appointed by the War Office. On the 1st of January, 1901, the territory was handed over to the control of the Colonial Office, and a Civil Commissioner assumed the administration of Wei Hai Wei in 1902.

The Civil Commissioner is appointed under the King's Sign Manual and Signet. By the Wei Hai Wei Order in Council of the 24th of July, 1901, he is empowered to make ordinances, subject to the approval of the Secretary of State for the colonies, for the administration of the territory, and provision is made for a High Court in which all jurisdiction, civil and criminal, is vested, subject to an appeal to the Supreme Court of Hong Kong, and for District Magistrates' Courts.

The village communities are administered through their headmen in accordance with Chinese customs.

Treaty Provision[②]

The treaty regulating the territory of Wei Hai Wei, signed on 1st July, 1898, specified that within the limits (285 sq·miles), Great Britain has the sole jurisdiction, except that within the walled city, Chinese officials may exercise such jurisdiction as is not inconsistent with naval

---

[①] Colonial Office List, 1914, p. 401; Directory and Chronicle for China, p.829.
[②] Hertslet, China Treaties, vol.1, p.122.

and military requirements for the defense of the territory leased.

With respect to the 1,505 sq. miles mutual zone, Chinese administration will not be interfered with, but no troops other than Chinese or British shall be allowed therein.

The first article provides that Great Britain shall lease this territory for so long a period as Port Arthur shall remain in the possession of Russia. Though Port Arthur was surrendered to the Japanese on January 1st, 1905, Great Britain has not indicated any intention to withdraw from Wei Hai Wei and an agreement was made between China and Great Britain whereby the latter is allowed to retain her lease for 25 years from the date of the signing of the Russian Treaty.

Port Edward

The chief port of the territory is named Port Edward in commemoration of the coronation of King Edward VII. This is a free port. Trade is carried on by junks and steamers. In 1912①, 632 steamers of 524, 927 tons entered the port, exclusive of admiralty colliers and were government transports; 452 were British and 180 were small Japanese and Chinese coasting boats. It is not destined to be a mercantile port.

---

① The Statesman's Year Book, 1914, p.180.

Wei Hai Wei as a Naval Base[1]

Although both Denby and Beresford have spoken highly of Wei Hai Wei as a naval base, yet the station has not been fortified. This is partly because of the Anglo–Japanese Alliance which, as was thought, renders fortification unnecessary and partly because Britain would not entail the heavy expenditure which the work requires. It is now used as a flying naval base and as a depot, exercising ground and sanitorium for the "China Squadron", which consists of 50 ships, and which assembles at Wei Hai Wei during the summer. No troops are stationed in this territory, the Chinese regiment having been disbanded. Military work cost Great Britain 130, 000 L in 1899. Since then this expenditure has not been made.

A Study of Finance in Wei Hai Wei

The revenue of Wei Hai Wei is drawn from land tax, road tax, Junk registration, shipping dues, wine monopoly, fines and miscellaneous sources. The revenue covers a little more than half of the expenditure; so the territory is not yet self-supporting. The deficit is made up by grant which is very small as compared with Germany's appropriation in Kiao Chow and Japan's appropriation in Kwantung. The annual revenue, expenditure, and grant are as follows[2]:

---

[1] The Statesman's Year Book, 1914, p.180.
[2] Figures of the years from 1903–13 are drawn from the Colonial Office List, 1914, p.401; from 1901–03, are drawn from Statesman's Year Book, 1906, p.195; from 1913–14, are drawn from The Statesman's Year Book, 1914, p.179.

Date	Revenue mix.dol.	Expenditure mix.dol.	Grant (£)
1901–02			11,250
1902–03			12,000
1903–04	58,364	166,921	9,000
1904–05	90,415	162,282	6,000
1905–06	105,934	146,120	3,000
1906–07	76,777	160,973	4,000
1907–08	80,331	173,341	10,000
1908–09	83,277	168,740	10,000
1909–10	83,499	145,687	4,000
1910–11	75,353	145,028	5,000
1911–12	14,673	153,591	6,000
1912–13	79,582	146,147	6,000
1913–14	72,436		8,300

Mining and Railway

Mining and railway enterprise are absent here. The territory contains gold, and a mining company has been working steadily for two years but has now ceased operation.[1] During the early German occupation of Kiao Chow, Great Britain consented by diplomatic agreement with Germany not to ask for any railway concession in the province of Shantung in order to avoid complications. This executive agreement has been observed.

---

[1] The Statesman's Year Book, 1906, p.195.

CHAPTER V WEI HAI WEI

The Importance of Wei Hai Wei to Great Britain

It is well known that Great Britain has the greatest amount of trade with China. Before the lease of Wei Hai Wei, the three principal ports along the northern coast of China were Chefoo, Tientsin, and Newchwang. According to the statistics of 1897[①], out of a total tonnage of 4,042,928 which cleared at the three ports, 2,265,658 tons were of British ships. The total trade of the three ports in 1897 was 103,469,664 hk.tls.[②], more than half of which was conducted by the British. British trade with Manchuria alone was then over £3,000,000. The distribution of tonnage entered and cleared at the three ports in the Gulf of Peichili in 1897 was as follows[③]:

Ports	Total tonnage of shipping entered and cleared	British tonnage entered and cleared
Chefoo	2,358,301	1,327,559
Newchwang	730,964	363,922
Tientsin	1326,663	574,177
Total	4,042,928	2,265,658

Such was the British trade in the Gulf of Peichili in 1897, a few months before the occupation of Wei Hai Wei. Without a naval station in the same water, British commerce would be at the mercy of Russia and Germany. Wei Hai Wei is important to Great Britain because it is thought to be the only safeguard for her commerce in northern China.

---

① Commercial Relations of the U.S, 1898 and 1899, vol. 1, under Chefoo, Newchwang and Tientsin.
② The approximate American equivalent of 1 hk.tls. in 1897 is $0.75.
③ Charles Beresford, The Break-up of China, Appendix, p 484

The Future of Wei Hai Wei

Great Britain justified her lease of this territory for the protection of commerce against the Russian lease of Kwantung and the German lease of Kiao Chow. Now both Kwantung and Kiao Chow have successively fallen into the hands of Japan, which is in alliance with Great Britain. Great Britain has abandoned her plan for the fortification of Wei Hai Wei because she thinks that the Anglo-Japanese alliance will render such a plan unnecessary. In theory, such a situation seems to be true; it seems that after Japan has got hold of Kwantung and Kiao Chow, Great Britain will no longer be in need of Wei Hai Wei. According to such a point of view, it will naturally follow that Great Britain will restore it to China as soon as the leased term expires. But is this the real situation? Have Great Britain's enemies in the China Sea disappeared with the fall of Kwantung and the fall of Kiao Chow? Is the Japanese alliance real and permanent? The destiny of Wei Hai Wei will depend to a large extent on these questions.

In every respect, Japan bears similarity with Great Britain. Both Japan and Great Britain are island countries. Both Japan and Great Britain are naval powers. Both Japan and Great Britain are manufacturing countries. Both countries have the same demands, same supplies, same ambitions, and same objects of contention. Their lending together into an alliance is only a matter of temporary convenience. Without going into the situation too deeply, let us review their struggle for commercial supremacy in China.

In 1909, British cotton goods trade with China covered ten-

CHAPTER V WEI HAI WEI

sixteenths of China's total importation of cotton goods[①], but decreased a great deal in 1910 and 1912. In spite of a little increase in the amount of this trade in 1913, importation of cotton goods in 1913 was nine to sixteen. During the same period, Japan's export of cotton goods to China increased from the ratio of one to sixteen to five to sixteen in 1913. Owing to the cheap labor in Japan and the shorter distance between Japan and China, Japan's advantage over Great Britain will become more marked as time goes on. This cotton goods trade is only typical; commercial competition between Japan and Great Britain is found in nearly every branch of trade. Mr. Weale says, "After having won the Russian War largely through Anglo–American moral support and Anglo-American gold, Japan intends to make profits and take payment, not from Russia, which remained unbeaten, but from the neutral world of Eastern Asia. In this contest, Japan will be a decisive factor along the vast Far Eastern coastlines, unless there is a naval combination of all Anglo-Saxondom."[②] Many English people have expressed such an opinion. At any rate, even those who have not gone so far as to show distrust in Japan, have doubt nevertheless in the so-called Anglo–Japanese Alliance which long ago lost the support of English public opinion. Great Britain leased Wei Hai Wei to counterbalance the influence of Russia and Germany. She is glad to see that both Russia and Germany have lost their influence in the Gulf of Peichili, but, contrary to her expectation, she has

---

① Under the name of cotton goods, the writer only includes shirtings, sheetings, drills, jeans T-cloths. The cotton goods trade of Japan Great Britain is as follows:Date Great Britain Japanpiecespieces190910, 691, 4481, 396, 29719106, 511, 1262, 389, 693191111, 317, 6302, 832, 62519129, 618, 3863, 043, 747191311, 705, 4265, 716, 594

② Weale, The Coming Struggle in Eastern Asia, p.519.

found a subtler competitor instead. It is not improbable that Wei Hai Wei will play a prominent part in future Anglo–Japanese relations.

So far as the trade in the North China Sea is concerned according to the statistics of 1911 and 1912, Great Britain still controls 11,000,000 of trade in Tientsin, Chefoo, Kiao Chow, and Newchwang, or about 40% of the total trade of the four ports. Tientsin in 1911 had a foreign net import of £7,098, 782 out of which 1,108,164 were British.[1] Newchwang in 1912, had a total import of £21,280, 721 out of which £453, 518 came from Britain.[2] Kiao Chow in 1911 had a total trade of £6,995,866, of which more than 60% of the cargo for Europe went in British bottoms.[3] Chefoo in 1912, had a total import of £672,353 of which, £276,615 was of British origin.[4] In a word, British trade in North China is still surpassed by none[5], and the safety of her trade in such places will depend to a large extent on Wei Hai Wei. This very fact will control the destiny of Wei Hai Wei at least for some years to come.

---

[1] House of Commons Sessional Paper 1912–13, vol.94, No.4902.
[2] Ibid, No.4901.
[3] Ibid, vol.95, No.4935.
[4] Ibid, 1912, No.5071.
[5] An exception is found in Dalny (Dairen) where Recording to 1912, British imports (including Hong Kong) represented only 6% while the Japanese imports into the said port were as high as 71.5%

CHAPTER VI

KOW LOON

CHAPTER VI KOW LOON

Kowloon, another English-leased territory, is situated around the ceded territory, Hong Kong. The extent of this territory is about 366 square miles, namely 286 sq ware miles on the mainland and 90 miles on the islands.① It comprises the territory behind Kowloon peninsula up to a line drawn from Mirs Bay to Deep Bay and the adjacent islands, including Lautao. It was leased to Great Britain on 9th June 1898.②

This territory is both important in itself and in its relation to Hong Kong. As to the value of itself, Mirs Bay, Deep Bay, Castle Peak Bay and Tolo Bay are good naval bases. The railway which passes through the mainland renders it a means of communication. With respect to its relation with Hong Kong, it furnishes type of the same type of protection to Hong Kong that he skull does to the brain. It is Hong Kong's background; it is Hong Kong's safeguard. In order to have a clear understanding of the importance of Kowloon, we must first have a real idea of how important Hong Kong is.

In speaking of the geographical situation of Hong Kong, one of the resolutions of the Hong Kong General Chamber of Commerce declares that Hong Kong, "lying halfway between India and Japan, on the very borders of one of the most populous provinces of China, and at the mouth of one of the greatest systems of inland navigation in Asia, is of supreme importance to British trade."

With respect to commerce, the same Chamber says, "The trade of Hong Kong, now（1898）roughly estimated at some fifty millions sterling per annum, may, when the river ways of South China are

---

① Directory and Chronicle for China, 1914, p.1108.
② Hertslet, China Treaties, vol. l, p.120.

opened and the railway to the Yangtze Valley becomes an accomplished fact, reasonably be expected to expand immensely." Taking the world shipping for comparison, Hong Kong today ranks as one of the greatest shipping centers in the world. The exact figures are:[1]

City	Tonnage entered and cleared (tons)
New York （1912）	13,673,763
Antwerp （1911）	13,330,699
Hong Kong （1912）	12,100,365
Hamburg （1911）	11,830,949
Rotterdam （1911）	11,052,186
Shanghai （1911）	9,429,996
London （1911）	9,004,974

According to the statistics of 1913[2], British imports from Hong Kong mount to £676,293, while her exports to Hong Kong mount as high as £4,358,902. This constitutes half of the total trade in Hong Kong.

Such has been the commercial condition of Hong Kong. The Chamber of Commerce in Hong Kong is not far from right when it declares, "However important the trade of the United Kingdom with central China, it must not be forgotten that the key to British influence and prestige in the Far East reposes in Hong Kong."

In regard to the sphere of influence, Hong Kong also furnishes a good starting point. The second resolution of the Hong Kong General

---

[1] Statistical Abstract, 1912, p. 815.
[2] The Statesman's Year Book, 1914, p.118.

CHAPTER Ⅵ　KOW LOON

Chamber of Commerce summarizes the situation as follows:

"Hong Kong, through a line of railway, connecting first with Canton, and eventually with Hankow and her sister cities Wuchang and Hanyang, is in a position to directly tap the very heart of commercial China."

It is the situation of Hong Kong that makes Kowloon important; it is the situation of Hong Kong that led Britain to lease Kowloon Instead of some other place.

Government

This new territory is administered by means of village communities organized, and under the direct control of of Hong Kong.① The headquarters of the administration are at Taipohu on an arm of Mirs Bay. A District Officer, who performs police and magisterial duties, resides there. The southern district is in charge of an assistant District Officer. In the treaty, a stipulation② was included that within the walled city of Kowloon the Chinese officials then stationed there should continue to exercise jurisdiction except so far as might be inconsistent with the military requirements for the defense of Hong Kong, but in 1899 the Chinese officials ceased to exercise jurisdiction within Kowloon city,

---

① The administration of Hong Kong is in the hands of a governor, aided by an Executive Council, composed of 6 official and 2 non-official members, three of whom are nominated by the Crown on the recommendation of the Governor, (two being usually Chinese),one is nominated by the Justices of Peace from their body and one by the Chamber of Commerce. The English Common Law forms the basis of the legal system, modified by Colonial Ordinances. See Colonial Office List, 1914, p. 211.

② Hertslet, China Treaties,vol. 1, p. 120.

which thereafter, by an Order in Council, was incorporated in the leased territory and became subject to British rule.①

Treaty Provisions②

The convention between China and Great Britain respecting the lease of kowloon, signed in on 9th June 1898, is similar to Wei Hai Wei treaty except in two respects. In the first place, the term of the lease of Kowloon is ninety-nine years instead of twenty-five years as is case of Wei Hai Wei. In the second place, we notice that there is a provision regarding railway construction in the Kowloon treaty, which is absent in that of Wei Hai Wei. It stipulates that "when hereafter China constructs a railway to the boundary of the Kowloon territory under British control, arrangements shall be discussed." This provision is exceedingly significant because through its application, the commercial value of Hong Kong has been safeguarded. The relation between the Kowloon–Canton Railway will command our immediate attention.

The Kowloon–Canton Railway

Why was the provision for this railway inserted in the Kowloon Convention? In 1897 when the Canton–Hankow section of the trunk line to Peking was projected and a concession granted to the American China Development Company, it was proposed to construct a deep water

---

① Colonial Office List, 1914, p.208.
② Herslet, China Treaties, p.120.

CHAPTER VI KOW LOON

harbor in the Chinese territory near Canton, the terminus. Hong Kong at once realised that if such a port were established and no effort made to secure the benefits of railway connection with trunk line, her existence as a distributing centre for south China would be threatened.[1] So great effort has been directed by British merchants and statesmen in securing the concession to build the line connecting Kowloon and Canton which, when completed, would provide the needed railway connection with the trunk line and thus preserve to Hong Kong at least her share of the trade even should the deep water harbor contemplated at Canton be realized. After securing the concession, the British and Chinese corporation was organized and after some delay, finally, in 1905, the corporation secured a loan of £1,500,000 from the Hong Kong Government and started its work. The line is in two sections. The first section between Canton and Shenchen (under Chinese control, but financed by the British Government) consisting of 89½ miles, is on Chinese territory. The section between Shenchen and Kowloon consisting of 22½ miles is on the leased territory. This line, after the Canton-Hankow railway (700 miles) has been completed, will not only have more immediate communication with the Yangtze Valley and Peking but will also furnish a serious check on the growth of Canton.

---

[1] The Far Eastern Review, 1909, Nov. No., p. 335.

CHAPTER VII

CONCLUSIONS

CHAPTER VII CONCLUSIONS

In the preceding chapters, the writer has attempted to give the actual facts concerning the territories leased by China to foreign powers. It now remains to compare the five leased territories, discuss the legal effects of the leases upon Chinese sovereignty over the territories, and present some general conclusions respecting the very intricate problems involved in this unique international situation.

Comparison of the Five Territories

In regard to the area of the leased territories proper, Kwantung stands first with an area of 1,256 square miles; next in order, follow Kowloon with an area of 366 square miles, Wei Hai Wei, with 285 square miles, Kiao Chow, with 193 square miles, and finally Kwang Chow Wan, with 190 square miles. Considered from the standpoint of present possessors, Japan controls the largest area, Kwantung and Kiao Chow with a total area of 1,449 square miles; Great Britain coming next has Wei Hai Wei and Kowloon with a total area of 651 square miles, and France coming last holds Kwang Chow Wan, 190 square miles.

With respect to the neutral zone, definite data is not obtainable for Kwantung. Both Kowloon and Kwang Chow Wan are devoid of neutral zones. Attaching to Kiao Chow, there is a neutral zone of 2,700 square miles and to Wei Hai Wei, one of 1,505 square miles.

In regard to population, the only place where the displacement of the Chinese by the lessee is felt is Kwantung. This may soon happen in Kiao Chow. There is nothing of this sort to be seen in Kwang Chow Wan, Kowloon, or Wei Hai Wei.

So far as the method of acquisition is concerned, after Germany had started the occupation of Kiao Chow, all followed one another and based their claims on the future protection of their own interests. Germany's motive and appearance as well as her action in acquiring Kiao Chow had been very open; every man knew her plan. Russia and France worked together; their words were sweet but their motives and actions, otherwise. However, men might still be able to tell their aims from their actions. There remained Great Britain whose words and actions all appeared to be courteous. An average man finds it very hard to tell whether Great Britain was true to the professions she made. At first, she sided with China to protest Russia's actions but she changed her course, joined in the spoliation and at last got two leases which were in total a greater territory except that gotten by the Russians. It might be claimed that Great Britain was justified in leasing Wei Hai Wei because it was necessary for her to protect her trade in north China against the Russians. But for what purpose was she persisting in demanding the lease of Kowloon? Someone says, "The lease of Kowloon was for the protection of Hong Kong." But against whom was the protection sought? Great Britain leased Wei Hai Wei for so long a period as Russia should retain her control over Kwantung. Why then should she like to retain Wei Hai Wei in spite of Russia's loss of Kwantung? With the recent Japanese demand for the extension of the lease of Kwantung to 99 years, will Great Britain herself take a similar step in regard to Wei Hai Wei? If Great Britain was sincere in her profession respecting the welfare of China, some concrete actions to that end will be acceptable. Finally, Japan's acquisition of Kwantung from Russia and Kiao Chow from Germany was prompted by her long cherished delusion of Continentalism; of course she hoped to justify her action by saying that

CHAPTER VII CONCLUSIONS 217

such measures guaranteed the peace of the Far East.

In considering the comparative commercial importance of these territories, Kowloon is prominent as the protector of Hong Kong, one of the world's greatest shipping centers. Dairen stands foremost in the rate of commercial growth. Kiao Chow is still the greatest among the leased territories in the amount of trade. Neither Wei Hai Wei nor Kwang Chow Wan have yet shown great commercial value.

Viewed from their naval value, Port Arthur in Kwantung is still the pioneer and surpassed by none in Chinese waters. Kiao Chow must be regarded as next in importance for naval operation. To the writer's mind, the natural position of Kowloon is far superior to any of the above-mentioned. This is but a personal opinion and it has by no means been proved by facts. Wei Hai Wei occupies a good position but it has not been fortified. Kwang Chow Wan is generally recognized as the least valuable naval base so far as the leased territories are concerned.

Finally, let us compare briefly the sphere of influence which each of the nations has planned to create in connection with these territories. In the creation of spheres of influence, railways are to be regarded as the chief agency. So a comparison of the railway system of each of them will give us both a general and definite idea of the situation. In this discussion, we must exclude Wei Hai Wei which has been incapable of developing a sphere of influence on account of the Anglo–German agreement. In connection with Kowloon, there is a railway line of 89 miles between Canton and Kowloon frontier financed and managed by English capitalists and engineers. Although this line is essential to the existence of Hong Kong yet as an agency for forming a sphere of influence, it is not very marked because the control is still in the hands of the Chinese government. A greater agency is found in the French line (248 miles), between Laokai and Yunnanfu in connection with the lease of Kwang Chow Wan. It is not until we come to Kiao Chow that we find something definite. The 310 miles of railway had been financed, controlled and managed by the Germans. Some definite German influence had been created along the railway lines. The sphere of influence remains in spite of the Japanese capture because Japan, as a victor, claims to inherit all rights and privileges which the Germans have enjoyed. The situation here has been well worked out but it is still in a milder stage. For the most conspicuous and most highly developed example we must turn to the sphere of influence in connection with Kwantung. Here the Japanese control a network of railways with a total trackage of 710 miles. The privilege of guarding the railway further strengthens her grip.

Legal Effects on the Sovereignty of China

In spite of all differences between these leased territories, there are some fundamental similarities in the conditions under which all of them are leased. They are all leased by treaties between the lessor and the lessee. This is even true in the case of transfer. They are all leased for a definite period of time. In all cases, China abstains from exercising the rights of administration during the term of lease. In all cases, China's men-of-war still have the right of station but they depend on the goodwill of the lessee. In all cases, the lessee has been given the right to build barracks and fortifications. Except Wei Hai Wei, all of them give some chances or other for the development of spheres of influence and

CHAPTER VII CONCLUSIONS   219

interest. Such are the general conditions under which the leases are made. What then are the legal effects upon the sovereignty of China over these territories?

In private law, the lease implies that property continues to belong to the lessor, while the lessee has the beneficial enjoyment of it for the time and under the conditions fixed in the contract. So when the property is granted in this manner, the original grantor retains a proprietary right which runs concurrently with the grantee's right of enjoyment. "Even when the lease is in perpetuity, that is an emphyteusis, the emperor Zeno decided that the lessor remains the dominus." Are we then to say that China still is sovereign over Kwantung, Kiao Chow, Wei Hai Wei, Kowloon and Kwang Chow Wan, though Japan, Great Britain, and France exercise, during the term of lease, important rights in them? In answering this questions we must first distinguish de jure sovereignty from de facto sovereignty.

From the de jure point of view, China exercises sovereignty over these territories not only after the expiration of the leases but also during the life of the leases. So with the Japanese capture of Kwantung and the ending of the Russian lease, China's consent was secured before the transfer had any legal force. And that consent was the evidence of China's sovereignty over it. The same thing is found in the recent transfer of Kiao Chow. Legally speaking, China's grant of rights of administration to the lessee is nothing but a delegation of powers, and the treaty of lease is only a matter of self-limitation. From the standpoint of international law, China is entitled to all rights pertaining to the owner of these territories on the conditions which she herself has set.

But owing to the relative weakness of China, this sovereignty only exists in a vague manner. As we come to the practical aspect, we note that her de facto sovereignty has been impaired. For example, all the lessees have acquired the power of unrestricted use of the soil for the erection of barracks, fortresses and other purposes as well warlike as pacific. Under such conditions, what then will be the relation between other powers and China with respect to their belligerent rights if they should be at war with China or with the lessee? If China were at war with other powers while the lessee remains as neutral, can the leased territory be regarded as a part of a belligerent zone? If one lessee were at war with other powers while China remains: neutral, can the leased territory be regarded as a part of the neutral zone? In theory, they ought to be but in practice, they are otherwise. The last case has been tried out both in the Russo-Japanese War and the Germane-Japanese war. Both of these occasions show conclusively that for all purposes of war and neutrality, leased territories formed a part of the domain of the lessee. In both cases either China's neutrality had been lost if she had de facto sovereignty over her leased territories or her de facto sovereignty had been impaired if her neutrality was regarded as unviolated, we may agree with Lawrence that in fact, the attempt to separate property or sovereignty on the one hand from possession on the other, by the use of phrases taken from the law of lease or usufruct, is in very nature deceptive. What China has really leased out is not only the territories but also the sovereignty thereover.

CHAPTER VII   CONCLUSIONS

Final Solution of the Leased Territories

What then is the final solution for the five leased territories? What shall the Chinese, the owners, do with the leases over which they are still supposed to have nominal proprietorship? Shall the Chinese finally waive their right over these territories as Sweden did over Wismar? Or shall they finally grant their leases in perpetuity as Zanzibar did in her dominion? Or shall the Chinese demand their restoration when the leases expire?

Attention is once more called to the fact that these territories are important front gates of China. China's gates must be kept by the Chinese. It is a great national crime for one nation to encroach upon another nation but it is still a greater national crime if a nation exposes itself as an international prey; such a nation not only endangers its own existence but also furnishes an incentive for international conflicts. Aliens, as gatekeepers for China, expose her to the avarice and ambition of aggressive and predatory peoples and therefore constitute a menace both to China and to the general peace and welfare of the world. For China and for the World, the Chinese have the supreme duty and mission of working toward the restoration of the territories they have leased. Restoration or downfall is the only alternative the Chinese have to choose.

Restoration depends on the unity of purpose, thought, and action for its realization. To determine the possibility of future success, we must first read the past. Many centuries ago, China built her "Great Wall", a wall which stretches from the farthest eastern coast to the farthest western boundary of China Proper, a wall which still stands and will ever stand with veritable pride, and a wall which defended her territory and people for generations. This reminds China of the possibility of building a "New Great Wall " to meet a new crisis. This "New Great Wall" will no longer be built with stone and brick, but will be built with four hundred million living bodies and souls united in one purpose. Such a "New Great Wall" is essential to the restoration of old territories; such a "New Great Wall" is essential to the prevention of international conflicts and the preservation of international peace in the Far East.

However, the restoration of the leased territories must not involve an anti-foreign movement. China must show herself broadminded, unprejudiced and friendly toward all nations, seeking nothing but her own national integrity and the preservation of peace.

China must recognize an obligation to humanity as well as to herself. Her national aims and policies will ultimately justify themselves only as they conserve the interests of mankind in general as well as China in particular.

In a word, Chinese territory and Chinese sovereignty should be maintained intact, and it lies with the present generation to recover the leased territories and restore Chinese sovereignty therein. Neutral nations should help to bring about this restoration because only by this act can the peace of the Far East be guaranteed, and the "Open Door Policy" be made effective. Interested nations should restore these territories to China because only by this act they can avoid conflict both with China and with one another. China must see to it and the world must understand that China has millions of square miles open for intercommunication but not one inch for occupation. Both must recognize that China's doors are to be widely open to welcome religion, art, science, and commerce but not a single door is to be opened for foreign political domination.

APPENDIX

A. BIBLIOGRAPHY
B. TABLE OF CURRENCY VALUES

A. BIBLIOGRAPHY

General

Cobbett, P. Cases and Opinions on International Law. Part 1. London, 1909.

Collection of Diplomatic Information (in Chinese). Shanghai.

Colquhoun, A. R. The Mastery of the Pacific, New York, 1904.

Commercial Relations of the United States. Washington, D. C. 1899–1912.

Directory and Chronicle for China, Japan, Straits Settlements, Indo-China, Philippines, etc. Hong Kong. 1914.

Douglas, Robert K. Europe and the Far East. Cambridge, 1904.

The Far Eastern Review. Nov. 1909. Shanghai, 1909.

Hart, A. B. The Obvious Orient. New York, 1911.

Hertslet, G. E. P. China Treaties. Vol. 1, Vol. 2. London, 1908.

Ireland, Alleyne. China and the Powers. Boston, 1902.

Ireland, Alleyne. The Far Eastern Tropics. Boston and New York, 1905.

The Japan Weekly Mail. Yokohama, 1897–99.

Kelte, J. Scott. The Statesman's Year Book, London, 1899–1914.

Krausse, A. The Far East. Its history and its questions. London, 1903.

Krausse, A: The Story of the Chinese Crisis, New York, 1900.

Lawrence, T. J. The Principles of International Law. New York, 1910

Michael, J, P. McCarthy, The Coming Power. London, 1905.

Monthly Consular and Trade Reports of the United States. Washington, D. C. 1899–1913.

Morris, H. C. The History of Colonization. vol.2. New York, 1900.

Morse, H. B. The Trade and Administration of China. New York, 1913.

Oppenheim, L. International Law. vol. l. New York, 1905.

Perrinjaquit, J·Des Cessions Temporaires des Territories.Paris, 1904.

Pinon, R. La Lutte Pour le Pacifique. Paris, 1912.

Presidential Message and Foreign Relations. Washington, D. C, 1901.

Reinsch, P. S. Colonial Administration. New York. 1905.

Reinsch, P. S. Colonial Government. New York. 1911.

Reinsch, P.S. World Politics. New York, 1900.

Tardieu, F. France and the Alliances. New York, 1908.

Weale, Putman. The Truce in the East and Its Aftermath. London.1907.

Westlake, K. C. International Law. Part 1. Cambridge, 1910.

Woodhead, H. G. and Bell, H. T. M. The China Year Book. New York, 1912–14.

Kiao Chow

Cheradame, Andr. La Colonisation et les Colonies Allemandes. Paris, 1905.

Garels, Karl.Deutsches Kolonialrecht. Giessen. 1902.

Gracey, W. T. German Government's Afforestation Work.

Washington. D.C., 1910.

Great Britain Foreign Office Reports. Nos. 549, 2758, 2790, 2983, 3296, 3519, 4508, 4682, 4935.

Grotewold, von Chr. Unaer Kolonialweser. Stuttgart, 1908.

Journal of the American Asiatic Association. New York, 1915.

Keller, A.G. Colonization. New York, 1908.

Loeh, Isidore. The German Colonial Fiscal System.

Mirbt, C. Mission und Kolonial Politik. Mohs, 1910

Outlook. November 11, 1914. New York, 1914.

Seidel, A. Deutschlands Kolonien. Berlin, 1909.

Tonnelat, E. L'Expansion Allemande hors D'Europe. Paris, 1908.

Verhandlungen des Deutschen Reichstags. Berlin, 1899–1913.

Kwantung

Deutsches Handels Archiv. 1912. Part 2. Berlin, 1912.

Great Britain Foreign Office Reports. Nos. 2832, 2999, 3144, 3348, 3681, 4206, 4372, 4504, 4789, 5023.

Krausse, A. Russia in Asia. New York, 1899.

Lawton, Lancelot. The Empire of the East. vol. 2. Boston.

Millard, T.F. America and the Far Eastern Questions. New York, 1909.

Takenos, Y. The Japan Year Book. Tokyo, 1908–14.

Weale, Putman. The Coming Struggle in Eastern Asia. London, 1909.

Kwang Chow Wan

Chambre des Députes; Budgets Locaux des Colonies. Paris, 1899–1914.

Cunningham, A. The French in Tonkin and South China. London, 1902.

Great Britain Foreign Office Reports. Nos. 2838, 2966, 3181, 3378, 3528, 3676, 3707, 3732, 4317, 4478, 4596, 4806, 4854, 4883.

Wei Hai Wei and Kowloon

Colonial Office List. London, 1911–14.

House of Commons Sessional Paper: Numerical List of command.

Colonial Reports of Great Britain. London, 1900–13.

B. TABLE OF CURRENCY VALUES

Chinese haikwan tael (hk. tl.) , fluctuate $0.70

English pound sterling (£) $4.94

French franc $0. 19

German mark $0.23

Japanese yen $0.49

French piaster...$0.48

Russian rubble $0.51